Praise for *So You Wanna: Start a Food or Beverage Business*

"Douglas knows what he's talking about. He's been through the ups and downs of the industry and seen all the major consumer shifts."
—Matt Matros, Founder of Protein Bar, Limitless, and Shopflix Studios

"Douglas speaks the truth, like it or not. The consumer packaged goods industry is a seven-days-a-week business. It is where the tough get knocked down and the tougher never get up. Success in this game is part luck, part timing, and part ride or die. Douglas captures this like the pirates before him."
—Thad Benshoof, CPG Investor and Cofounder of Homegrown Meats

"This is far from your typical business book and will undoubtedly keep readers engaged and inspired as they choose their own unique path to starting a business. Like life itself, nothing is linear, and Douglas does a fantastic job at giving readers a tangible road map of how to find success and persevere as an entrepreneur."
—Sara Brooks, Founder of Covet PR

"Douglas Raggio has written a book that is uniquely packed with practical and no-nonsense advice for aspiring entrepreneurs. Interlacing his own experience as a VC and a start-up founder, Douglas presents case studies of how four real-life entrepreneurs tackled critical issues that all start-ups face. Uniquely written and organized to give the reader an interactive experience, *So You Wanna* is not only instructive but highly entertaining."
—Chris L. Shimojima, Founder & President C5 Advisory

"A lot of folks wonder about starting a food or beverage company. While it can be incredibly rewarding, it can also be a treacherous, circuitous path fraught with peril. Douglas Raggio shares hard-won lessons and practical nuts-and-bolts advice that improve your odds and can help make your dream a reality."
—Bob Burke, 25-year consultant, advisor, and board member at Natural Products Consulting, LLC,

"This is one of those books that is mandatory reading before starting a CPG company. It will save you hundreds of thousands of dollars in mistakes. It is real and researched through the eyes of people that have been there and done that."
—Nick Saltarelli, Cofounder of Mid-Day Squares

"I can't think of anyone better to lay out a path for food and beverage start-up success. Douglas's experience as an entrepreneur and investor puts him in a unique position to support your growing, young company and the book's unique layout makes it simple for you to get just what you need out of it. Absorb the lessons in this book, apply them, and watch your business succeed!"

—Robert U. Craven, Managing Partner of Findaway Adventures
and former CEO of MegaFood and Garden of Life

"If you've ever thought about launching your own food or beverage business, this book's for you. It offers readers an interactive journey through the unforgiving trenches of the start-up world. Raggio's raw and witty prose makes each path feel all too real as you cling to this unexpected page turner. The twists and turns will leave you questioning your own motives and whether or not you've got the grit needed to succeed."

—Brittany Callahan, food and beverage start-up curious

"I have talked to thousands of founders over the past two decades during their journey of starting a food or beverage company and continue to be humbled by the complexities that must be navigated unique to each brand. The more founders can learn early on, the more they can grow their brands by avoiding costly mistakes that consume capital. This book is a great source of practical information for early-stage founders."

—Nick McCoy, Cofounder and Managing Director of Whipstitch Capital

"Read this book if you want an exhilarating, adrenaline rush, filled with decisions that only you can make. Adventures await!"

—Jessica Ann, author of *Humanize your Brand*

So You Wanna:

START A FOOD OR BEVERAGE BUSINESS

So You Wanna:

START A
FOOD OR
BEVERAGE
BUSINESS

DOUGLAS RAGGIO
with Heidi Scott

Matt Holt Books
An Imprint of BenBella Books, Inc.
Dallas, TX

Matt Holt Books is an imprint of BenBella Books, Inc.
10440 N. Central Expressway
Suite 800
Dallas, TX 75231
benbellabooks.com
Send feedback to feedback@benbellabooks.com.

BenBella and *Matt Holt* are federally registered trademarks.

Printed in the United States of America
10 9 8 7 6 5 4 3 2 1

Library of Congress Control Number: 2021037221
ISBN 9781953295668 (trade cloth)
ISBN 9781637740002 (ebook)

Copyediting by Scott Calamar
Proofreading by Lisa Story and Dylan Julian
Text design and composition by PerfecType, Nashville, TN
Cover design by Brigid Pearson
Cover image © Shutterstock / MicroOne
Printed by Lake Book Manufacturing

*Mom & Dad—I can hardly express the sheer gratitude I feel
for your unwavering support as I found my way through every
misdirection of logic and errant pursuit. I love you.*

*My brother David—I admire how you do it all and the man you have
become with your family. I am honored you kept me around. I love you too.*

*Grandma—Getting to know you as an adult has been a highlight
of my life. So fun, so wise . . . You're a hoot to the highest degree
(and still the reigning best gift giver in the family). I love you.*

CONTENTS

INTRODUCTION

I'm jaded. In the many years I have been in this industry, I have met thousands of enterprising individuals with amazing food ideas for the consumer packaged goods (CPG) industry. I am always impressed with the scrappy, can-do attitudes they have, and I feel compelled to offer whatever wisdom I can to help them. Before I founded Pass the Honey, I'd probably vetted over 12,000 investment opportunities. Through that, I've seen a lot of business models and even more brand ideas. Because of this, I have a unique advantage in seeing what does and does not work for the most part. I can tell when a company has the potential for permanence and when it will flicker with the trends.

What I have written in this book are just my opinions, based on my experience. This is my attempt to shed some light on the not-so-rosy outcomes and decision-making that happens in this industry. Through my investment funds, both Gastronome Ventures and Bias & Blind Spots, I am regularly approached by people who ask my advice because they have a great product and think that is all it will take to hit the jackpot. Knowing of my experience in the food business, they hope I can steer them in the right direction. They mentally make the jump from concocting their new product idea in the kitchen to

1

seeing it in grocery stores across the country. What they don't see are the million little steps and missteps that happen in between.

There are many promising companies trying to squeeze into the almost magically rare path to success in this industry. This results in 98–99 percent of all new food businesses failing on some level, and many entirely giving up.

But while the numbers are definitely stacked against you as a start-up CPG business, there is always hope. Success doesn't have to be based solely on monetary measures.

Your North Star

Years ago I worked in the ER, so I'm accustomed to indicators and contraindicators when administering drugs. Indicators guide a health-care provider toward making a specific decision, while contraindicators provide reasons not to make decisions. Knowing what those are is paramount to your success in treating patients.

Similarly, when you start a business, it is essential to watch for indicators and contraindicators. These can be considered guardrails to keep you on the path you pick. If you decide you want a small business, something that is more of a hobby, and suddenly you have Costco knocking on your door and wanting to carry your product, the misalignment of the request with your goal is a contraindicator. It should raise a red flag to help you slow down before you make any rush decisions.

How do you define your personal North Star? By North Star, I mean what kind of life do you want? How do you define success? By the time you are finished reading this book, I hope you can sit down with a clear head and outline what you consider to be your fullest life.

Do you want to make just enough money to put your kids through college or buy a nice home? Not every business needs to be bought by an international behemoth. Or do you envision being on the global stage and challenging major conglomerates? Or maybe you simply want a quick exit after "only" five to eight years of your time. These are vastly different types of companies, so having a vision of where you are going from the beginning is essential. As your business ebbs and flows through success and failure, you need that North Star to guide your choices.

Throughout the growth process, you will be presented with tempting decisions that have the potential to knock you off your center. Regardless of your goal, I encourage you to maintain perspective while constantly checking your thinking. This is a game of perspective filled with opportunities that seem realistic but may easily be red herrings that throw you off your course. The key is to keep your eye on your foundational goals. What, exactly, is it you want to achieve? DO NOT lose sight of that.

You may find that a small, manageable farmers' market presence is enough for you to meet your goals. You may decide that having the capacity to produce your product for two or three local stores is as far as you want to go, and that makes you happy. Or you may even be one of those whose company is acquired one day by a global food conglomerate (only if that's your North Star).

Proceed with Caution

This book is a meant to be a cautionary tale and a warning to all who think that because they have a fabulous cookie recipe or a new smoothie idea, they are going to make millions in a year or two. That fantasy is not only unrealistic, it is virtually impossible. Far too often we get caught up in the fever of a new idea and forget that we must stop and really look at what the future holds. Sometimes we don't see that we are following the false positive of encouragement from friends and family, while in the end, the juice just isn't worth the squeeze. Ultimately, the point of this book is to encourage you to stop and think before you do anything else.

Anyone who has been told that they really ought to take their home-baked dessert, homemade salad dressing, or whatever and go into business selling them to the general public will hopefully find this book to be an indispensable guide.

Sometimes it's worth pausing for a moment, putting some critical thinking to work, and understanding what you, as a potential founder, want out of life and out of your business. What are your expectations? What assumptions are you working with? Contemplate what resources you have access to and which ones you don't. What is unique to your brand? (Hint: it can't be taste because that's subjective, and it can't be better ingredients because those are always evolving.) So what else? What else can you defend? What else can you build value around?

Now, take a moment to ask yourself why you're moving forward with your idea. Not just because a friend told you it tasted good and not just because you think it's a fun hobby. If you haven't ever articulated the reason, this book is for you. Just because you have a good brownie doesn't mean you have a good business.

You may have discovered that there are lots of general books about being an entrepreneur and what it takes to succeed in a difficult and challenging business environment. But the truth is, very few of those books are specific to packaged food and beverages.

Sometimes I wish I didn't know as much as I do about the food business. Most of what you read in this book springs from my own experience. To learn more about how I arrived at the specific numbers you will see, I refer you to two excellent resources with powerful visuals: a 2018 CBInsights article titled "Venture Capital Funnel Shows Odds of Becoming a Unicorn Are About 1%" and a January 25, 2017, PitchBook article titled "3 charts that show the effect of venture fundraising on founder ownership" by Adley Bowden.

I used to believe that blind faith and grit meant things would work out. Sadly, they do not. That old adage rings true: "If I knew then what I know now, I wouldn't have started." And it's expensive learning. Rather than keeping my expertise limited to coffee and lunch meetings, I'll put it in writing.

I'll be the first to say that there are far too many brands out there. Too many people get into this business when they shouldn't. You see it for yourselves on the shelves. Do we really need a hundred different energy bars? Maybe. Most likely not.

What's the big difference between them all? It's not only taste. They're roughly the same bar and the same flavors in the same sizes. How many different ways can we use peanut butter and chocolate? And then you start getting the exotics, the turmeric and the goji berries and the hemp seed. It's just an endless iteration on a standard form. This is what's referred to as a cluttered or crowded category.

I firmly believe our industry needs more category creators. You get Chobani bringing Greek yogurt into the yogurt aisle, and suddenly it's a differentiator. It stands out. You get an energy bar that's placed in the fridge instead of on the shelf or you're putting refrigerators in the baby food aisle, and suddenly that's a unique take on an established category.

But those types of decisions are the longer, harder paths. They're also the decisions that create some longevity and some permanence. My focus as an investor, after a brief stint as a short-sighted VC (venture capitalist), is to create permanence in our food supply and establish brands with legacy.

Pick Your Own Path

Something I always enjoyed as a kid were the "choose your own adventure" type books. I liked going back and forth while I read, trying a new path to see how different choices would make the story end. As I contemplated writing this book, I couldn't help feeling that this format was very applicable in a business-style book. In business, the subtle decisions made early on can lead to vast success or significant failure down the line.

In the following pages, I will introduce you to a cast of four characters who represent standard archetypes of people starting food and beverage companies. There are many differences in how these businesses get going. Sometimes you have a unique or better product that you developed on your own and now you want to sell it. Sometimes you have a really great idea and now you have to figure out how to make it.

Hopefully you'll see a bit of yourself in one or more of these characters and be able to learn vicariously through their successes and missteps. At each juncture, you'll be faced with a decision that will take contemplation and critical thinking. Put yourself in the shoes of the character and see if you can get them to their goal.

You will hit dead ends. I've also invited real brand-name founders to weigh in and offer their personal stories about how similar decisions were made in real life and the results of those choices. You'll see how very rare it is to have a product become a household, global brand while retaining independence and freedom. (Hint: that rarely happens.)

There is no one set path to success. Period.

I do find it incredibly ironic that so many founders idolize the Chobanis and Patagonias of the world, yet so few actually follow those pathways because it takes a ton of time. And we've got this instant gratification society that just wants to create this *now*. We've got these synthetic, ether-driven brands that are launched off Instagram and a couple of followers, and there's no merit to them. However easy it may be, it isn't the best way to build permanence, because the next person can come and do the exact same thing. There's a very low bar for entry. You may be surprised that by the end of this book, you won't have any concrete "how to" steps or easy answers. What you will have is the slight advantage of knowing the types of decisions you'll be making day in and day out.

After all, the definition of "success" is up to you. My goal is to help you go into your start-up with eyes wide open, knowing the stumbling blocks that will inevitably come your way. My decades of experience have proven that while every start-up is unique, there are predictable patterns that we can depend on. My hope is that after reading this book, you will be armed with knowledge and have a plan in place to tackle hiccups when they come. I want you to make the very best decisions for yourself and for your company as you do (or don't) start a food business.

So, without further ado, good luck. And I'm rooting for you.

INSTRUCTIONS FOR READING THIS BOOK

STOP! READ THIS FIRST!

This book isn't meant to be read front to back. In fact, if you try, it will quickly become nonsense.

In this book, just like in real life, you are responsible for the direction of your journey. The pages ahead offer many pathways. As you read, you will be stopped and asked to pick a direction, and then you'll turn to a certain page to continue the journey based on that choice. Each choice may lead to success or failure.

Throughout the book, I have sprinkled quotes and case studies from real-life founders who have been there and done that and learned the hard way. Unlike real life, in this book there are redos. If you reach an ending that isn't satisfying, you can (and should) go back to the previous decision and pick a different path.

I have designed this book in such a way that you will inevitably make mistakes and end up at dead ends that force you to revisit the decisions you previously made. As you pick alternative paths to explore, you'll discover that, like life and business, there is no magic formula. The hope is that as you double back to the same path more than once, you will consider how similar this is to life.

Of course, I couldn't possibly take you down every possible path in the CPG business. And I don't want to. As you pick your own path, think about what might happen in your own unique circumstances. Perhaps a dead end for our character would actually be a turning point to success for you.

There are commonalities in the process for everyone in the food and beverage industry. Paths to marketing are very similar regardless of product category. I hope you pick up on nuances. This experience is simply meant to help you find your identity. To give you space to contemplate. To ask questions. And to peel back the layers.

Remember, there is no such thing as perfection in the world of business, and no single path to success. There is no template, and anyone who says there is should be handled with a healthy measure of skepticism.

You're in the business of trade-offs and quick decisions with partial information. That is the reality. And, like real life, you have to use what you do know to make the best decision you can, understanding that it will likely change tomorrow. There are unintended consequences—some will be beneficial and some will not. There are tough calls and compromises.

And that, my friend, is what business is all about.

Have fun!

THE
Archetypes

In the CPG world, I have found most founders fall into one of four basic categories. I created these archetypes based on amalgamations of real founders I know.

These descriptions of each archetype should give you enough information to make a choice on where to start. You will learn more about each character after you turn to their story. Consider starting with the person who most closely resembles you and following their path first, and then coming back to the others. As you read, you'll notice some repetition of paths between the characters as their decisions intertwine. This is on purpose and reflects how most CPG founders face similar experiences as they travel down this path.

Side note: I recognize that working with a partner or multiple partners is a common occurrence in food business. For the scope of this book, each of these characters is working as an individual founder. But if you are considering going into business with someone else, be it family, friend, or acquaintance, I strongly encourage you to read the "Real Founders: Partnerships" section at the back of the book.

Angela

Angela is a single mother of two teenage daughters. She works in corporate America as a project manager. By all measures, she is a great earner because she does everything by the book and is an amazingly driven individual. This approach has led to a decent savings above and beyond her retirement and investment accounts, somewhere between $30,000 and $40,000. Her greatest desire is to provide a comfortable life for herself and her daughters in the future.

When one of her daughters was young, Angela learned that she was severely allergic to many typical ingredients found in most prepackaged baked goods. Rather than watching her go without the same treats her sister enjoyed, Angela set out to make something they could all enjoy together that would not trigger an allergic reaction. She sourced ingredients from three different stores in town and some online vendors to ensure they were the highest quality.

After much experimentation, she created a "free-from" muffin that tasted great while being free from allergens such as dairy, eggs, nuts, soy, and gluten. Through the years, she shared her "free-from" muffins at her office, her girls' school events, and with friends and family. She has been constantly told that they are so good she should sell them. She even came up with a nickname for them, YesMuffins, because everyone she knew could say yes to eating them.

As time went on, her daughter took them to school and sporting events. She'd toss them in her lunch sack and sometimes swap them with her friends. Angela always opted in to every event that asked for food donations, because she knew her daughter wasn't the only person with food allergies. Her driving force is giving every person the ability to experience joy in food without having to worry about a reaction.

Angela really enjoys making and sharing her YesMuffins. She shares her recipe online with other parents who have children with severe allergies. She discovered that her recipe appeals to people with more than just allergies—it also fits other dietary restrictions, including those in vegan and keto diets.

Locally, she is known for the YesMuffins. But Angela's fatal flaw is that she's easily influenced. She can't help listening to what everyone says. When she shows up with a plate of muffins, people flock to her. When they find out they're free-from, they all say the same thing: "It doesn't even taste like that! You should make a business out of this. I'd totally buy these if you made them!"

At one point a few years ago, she really was tempted to go into business. She even started looking into special bags to put them in and thinking about competition. But she decided against it. She's so busy with her job and raising her daughters that starting a business never felt like a good idea. She just doesn't have much time to give.

Angela brings passion, personal connection, and overwhelmingly positive feedback. She also has enough business acumen and project management experience through her day job that she feels confident that she can handle starting a new venture. She knows she has a built-in client base with those who follow many different diets, including keto, vegan, and carnivore.

Angela doesn't know much about the food space, but she is very confident in her own abilities to manage projects and get things done. She is dedicated and vigilant, so she has faith in herself that she can create a business. What she lacks in investment dollars, she is confident she can make up for in wisdom and enthusiasm.

 PROS Success, project management, available finances, passion, encouragement

 CONS Easily influenced, lacks marketing knowledge, time

Nathaniel

By all accounts, Nathaniel is a handsome gent. He's tall, lean, and fit. But he had a very different body type when he was younger. He used to be a food addict who "ate his feelings." In his early twenties, he began having some health issues that traditionally would be attributed to somebody twice his age.

Under encouragement from his family, he went to a wellness camp where he detoxed and learned to take on a healthier diet and exercise. This experience transformed his life and broke his addiction to the unhealthy junk foods he had come to depend on. He went on to become a marketer by trade and gained incredible skills in social media engagement.

His personal journey of learning how to heal himself with food is an integral part of his identity. In fact, he has that deep connection to food that heals the body and mind and soul, so he has more of a philosopher's take on it. His first product (of many, he hopes) is a healthy alternative to the sugary sodas he used to guzzle. And he wants to see his high-quality product on the shelves of convenience stores marked at prices comparable to other junk foods.

As he's connected with others in his profession, he finds that he enjoys sharing his story about healing himself with better food. His ambitions and intentions are based purely on his desire to help others.

Nathaniel has this great personal story and a great connection with others. In fact, his audience is growing by the day. He's very engaging and knows how to reach into the internet and find loyal customers.

The idea for his product came when he failed to find an existing product that could relieve his occasional urge for a sugary beverage. He developed an energy drink called ExtraMetaNomNom that is, in his opinion, just the right combination of superfoods and sweetness. He believes this to be the answer to the world's soda addiction.

His passion grows into a desire to eclipse the world's biggest beverage companies with his brand. It mimics the taste and experience of the most unhealthy drinks, but in a healthful, clean manner. Unfortunately, his ambitions and his ability to fund and manage this business don't match. He comes from a family of impact investors, so he's on his way, due to their support. But their funds are running out, and he really wants to do it on his own, without having to take money from anyone else.

His goal is to create a global brand at global brand prices, but with fresh food costs that are quadruple what those global brands use, and that's where it gets tough. He wants to help people make better choices by giving them a healthy alternative at the same prices they're used to. Excellent. That's like the Holy Grail of CPG. Everybody wants that.

There are plenty of healthy, big brands at affordable prices, but they didn't start out that way. To come roaring out of the gate with this ambition to build for scale on a shoestring budget just doesn't really align.

Nathaniel is quite young but is well funded for someone his age due to family connections. Additionally, he has partnerships with large organizations with a health focus, which gives him a leg up.

 PROS Marketing savant, young, personal story, access to funding

 CONS Trying to build scale fast without giving up control, better quality at low prices (access)

Veronica

Veronica was raised in a healthy home in a mild climate, so her family grew much of their produce in a little garden in the backyard. She grew up accustomed to quality ingredients in vibrant, made-from-scratch meals. From a very young age, she loved spending time hip-to-hip at the kitchen counter with her mother and grandmother, cooking and tinkering with recipes until they were just right. Because of this, she was an absolute natural in terms of living a healthy, clean lifestyle.

In her early twenties, Veronica became an endurance athlete and ultrarunner. When she suffered from leg cramps early in her training, a seasoned ultrarunner turned her on to pickle juice. She was surprised and thrilled to find that not only did it work, but also there were single-serve bottles on the market that she could take with her on her long runs.

The problem came in trying to fit those bottles into her running vest along with all the energy-boosting, protein-packed snacks she needed to sustain her energy. She and all of her running companions carried water and bars and gels and powders and chews, so they didn't have space for the pickle juice bottles.

At this time, she was going through her MBA program and had to come up with a thesis project. She decided to try to solve the problem she was facing by combining everything she needed during a long run into one package. She fortified pickles to include more juice for cramps, electrolytes for replenishment, and added protein to sustain energy. She tinkered around in her tiny apartment kitchen and finally came up with Perfect Power Pickles. They ticked all the boxes she needed, in addition to being nutritious, delicious, and vegan.

While she was getting her MBA, she created a type of protein-packed pickle that all her roommates loved. Word spread fast and it wasn't long before she began selling her pickles to fellow students out of her apartment.

The running community is really tight, so she shared them with fellow runners. They got really excited, and it wasn't long before she had requests from people she knew and even some she didn't asking if they could buy Perfect Power Pickles before every race. She lost count of how many times she heard people say, "You really should make a business out of this because these are great!"

From that, her pickles became a known commodity. She started with a crack crew of herself and a few devoted friends on weekends making them and packaging them in homemade bags. She got contracts with a couple of local running stores to carry them, and they sold out regularly. She even developed a variation with exactly 15 grams of added carbs for her diabetic boyfriend for when he needed to bring up low blood-sugar levels.

With her fresh education in finance and business analysis, she realized that her product had the potential to be a behemoth. She had success at the outset. Today, Veronica has an original, patented recipe for Perfect Power Pickles with a large and loyal customer base, albeit local. Her creativity has the potential to upset an entire category and could knock some of the old incumbents with really crappy products off the shelves by bringing something unique and novel to the marketplace. In just a few years, her pickles have gained local attention from farmers' markets and independent regional retailers. She's got investors asking, "Hey, do you want to take this thing to the next level?"

Friends and family are also wondering if they can invest in her company, and she is excited at the idea of creating something that she is incredibly passionate about. She is really tempted to accept the first money that is offered.

 PROS Success, customers, global brand opportunity, rapid growth, agile

 CONS Taking first money offered, running fast, no precedent to learn from

Being a category creator can be both good and bad.

Charles

Charles has been in the industry for over a decade. A seasoned CPG man, he became disenchanted with the ways food companies were being run. He did not agree with their model and sought for a way to create permanence and independence in the CPG industry. He understands the trade deeply because of past experiences, failing and succeeding to a certain degree with other ventures.

A number of years ago he took a humanitarian trip to Ghana and witnessed firsthand the poverty that cacao producers lived in. He learned that growers were poorer now than they were decades ago due to unfair labor practices. He also witnessed the negative ecological impacts of the slash-and-burn practices cacao famers used to clear land. He was moved to do something that would make a difference.

This is when he came up with the idea for Truth in Cacao, a company focused on addressing the problems he witnessed. In addition to his desire to create a legacy company, he wanted to ensure fair labor practices and sourcing at the highest standards. Additionally, he intends to invest back into the supply chain for a broader impact on global economic and environmental health.

Having been raised in a family involved in activism, social justice, and equality, the fair-trade component was on his mind. He wanted to get clarity on the problem. He dug a little deeper and learned that cacao is one of the more poorly traded, poorly regulated food commodities.

He saw the explosion of healthy food and could see the juxtaposition between how food companies were perceived before and how food companies are perceived now. He understands the function of venture capital, cash flow, cost of goods, sales channel, and diversification. He has been around long enough to witness the stumbling blocks of other founders and, to a large degree, is confident he has learned enough to hopefully avoid many of those common missteps.

Charles knows enough to be dangerous, as they say. He is an idealist and has an idea about how businesses should be running that is very counter to what is currently happening in the food and beverage space. He does not like the prevailing philosophy of growing a company to sell. That does not vibe with him.

It takes a different kind of capital to do what he wants to do. It takes a different kind of investor. It's almost like building things in a completely opposite way to how everyone else is building them. He wants to swim upstream against the tide and counter to where the rest of the fish are going.

He's willing to make the sacrifices because he's doing something new. He doesn't mind being an island. The structure and the impact of his company are different and new. He is not trying to just sell it in five years, which is what everyone else expects. He anticipates that he will have to provide a little bit more explanation to people as part of the process of creating something that is unfamiliar.

He coupled his vision of how he can change the food industry from within with his desire to clean up the specific commodity class. Cacao is a premium item, which allows the ability to actually charge a little bit more so that he can reinvest in the supply chain. But he has to educate his consumers. He has to let them know that what they're buying has traditionally come from some pretty poor labor practices and has had a negative ecological impact. So, he is altruistic in that regard.

But due to his background, Charles has a little bit of a chip on his shoulder. He sees a lot of the industry as being wrong. He's an idealist who thinks things should be done in different ways. He wants food businesses to run properly and have some sort of permanence.

Because what Charles is doing has never been done before, he is having to figure things out as he goes. There is no clear path to success laid out before him. His goal is to build a company that is defendable to potential investors, has the proper margins, and can sell product at a high enough rate to be sustainable. He wants to create a company that lasts a century.

 PROS Experience, knowledge, resources in space, funding (sort of)

 CONS Too knowledgeable, chip on his shoulder, "us vs. them" mentality

Decision: Which character do you identify with?

To pick **Angela**, turn to page 23

To pick **Nathaniel**, turn to page 61

To pick **Veronica**, turn to page 111

To pick **Charles**, turn to page 169

Angela's
PATH

You Are Now Angela

You get so much repetitive feedback for your YesMuffins that, even though you're smart enough not to believe everything you hear, you start to wonder if there's really an opportunity here. You know there are laws in every state regarding home-baked goods that provide people like you with the ability to produce goods up to a certain scale. This could be a great side business and provide a little supplemental income.

You have that nice little savings account waiting for a rainy day. You can't help wondering, "Could I really get this going? I buy more ingredients each time I shop and make more muffins. How hard could it be?"

You are definitely passionate about your recipe and the joy it brings to others, but one thing is certain: You are not interested in taking anything too far. You have no interest in being a global brand, or really even a regional brand.

Maybe you'll make enough to send your kids through college or maybe just enough to take one nice trip every year. That's sufficient. You enjoy baking YesMuffins. You enjoy sharing them. If this made maybe six figures a year, you'd feel amazing.

When you pick Angela's path, you as a founder have many opportunities to stay in control of your destiny because you have the chance to either opt for large-scale production or keep it small and maintain a healthy work/life balance. There isn't any unnecessary complexity because you're not forced into any decisions. But if you're easily influenced—like Angela is—you are your own worst enemy.

So the first decision that you face is: Do you choose to listen to the positive feedback you keep getting? Your time and money may be best served elsewhere. You may also want to take a crack at owning your own destiny.

Decision: Do you decide to start a food business?

To **not start a business**, turn to page 25

To **start a business**, turn to page 27

Congratulations! You just saved yourself a lot of time and stress.

There is no shame in deciding it's not worth your time. Sometimes the juice just isn't worth the squeeze. There are opportunity costs with everything. And a minimum of $300,000 from your savings and loans from friends and family. Did you know it typically takes between $300,000 and $700,000 to actually get a company off the ground and functioning in the food space? The amount of money needed can go up to a million or two. I've even heard of founders using $5 million to get their ideas off the ground.

As a side note, many seasoned CPG executives believe that a company cannot generate a profit until it brings in $100 million in revenue. I was told this by one of my own advisors. But it is simply untrue. You always have to consider the source. That advisor's background was creating venture and private equity–backed big brands. He is really good at spending tons of cash fast. That's what he is hired to do. In that scenario, his belief is correct, but that is not the path for everybody else.

All that said . . .

With this decision, you have a happy life. You continue to make and share your free-from muffins, and when people say, "You should totally make these for the stores. I would buy them!" you just smile and know that you've made your choice.

There are plenty of businesses I should have never started in my own career. In hindsight, they did not reflect my passion. They were opportunistic in nature, just looking for quick money, which never ends well for me. I don't have the engine to get through the tough days. In the end, they aren't worth my time or my money. I don't regret these, though, because of the lessons learned.

THE
END

Or not?

Here's the thing. Your decision will nag at you. And because it nags at you, when your friend asks if he can take you to lunch, and then offers to partner with you in this free-from muffin business, you reconsider. In general, I advise you to be cautious before you partner with friends or family. It ends poorly far too often. I really hope you read the appendix at the end of this book called "Real Founders: Partnerships" to get advice from people who have had a variety of experiences working with others.

It doesn't take long before you change your mind. You were confident at one point in your decision to say no, but suddenly another person believes in you. It becomes tempting again.

This is really common, actually. When you have a great product or mission, people who know you want to join. This can be a great thing. You don't have to be the only one doing all the work. Partners will have skills you don't have and will break up the workload. They can also hold you accountable, which can be appealing. Suddenly the idea of starting a food business doesn't seem so insurmountable anymore.

To **start a business**, turn to page 27

You feel brave and bold and ready to take on the world. You are confident that your product will sell because of how many people have told you they will buy it. You step out into the world of CPG with excitement.

Now that you've decided to make a go at this, you have to figure out how to make enough muffins to sell. If you stay at home, you can save costs and do it whenever you are in the mood. A good friend of yours told you that some people use what is called a shared kitchen, and that sounds interesting.

As you research shared kitchens (also referred to as commercial kitchens), you learn that you have to schedule in advance. You know they are just a little more complicated in terms of logistics, but it would give you the ability to make a lot more muffins in less time. Not to mention the mess it would save in your home.

But then again, you're not sure if you want this to be a full business or not. You're still exploring.

All that said . . .

Your friend is supportive of anything you want to do but doesn't have any experience or even any opinions to help you. You have to decide where to make your muffins based on the little you currently know. You heard a rumor there might be a few shared kitchens in your community, but you don't even know where to find them.

You might want to save some money and make muffins at your leisure or spend a little and start scheduling with a shared kitchen.

Decision: Do you continue to make your product at home, or do you find a shared kitchen?

To **stay at home**, turn to page 29

To **find a shared kitchen**, turn to page 33

You keep on using your own kitchen. Cooking at home gives you the freedom and flexibility to produce your muffins at your leisure, be it late nights after work or weekends when you just want to be in the kitchen.

But there are challenges. There are space constraints, so you can only cook so many muffins at a time. Rarely have I seen a house that has three ovens or more. There's no storage for ingredients, and your mixer is always on the counter with your muffin tins, and you had to find a special gate to keep your dog far away from the kitchen because it's spring and she's shedding. So you are finding your life revolving around the muffins.

It's also getting expensive because you have to continue to buy all your ingredients from your retail sources, at whatever retail prices happen to be at the time. You are able to find online sources to help with some of the ingredients, but to keep the integrity of the product, you don't want to change the recipe.

You would like to buy in bulk so you can get discounts on ingredients, but you also have a pantry that's only so big. And that pantry already has your family's food in it. Should you buy a second fridge for the garage? Or build more shelving in your kitchen? What happens when you need the kitchen to make a dinner for guests, but everything is tied up in your muffins? This image might be romantic in your twenties, but not so much when you are in your forties with a family.

Not to mention the time it takes. Now when you want to come home after a long day at work and relax in front of the TV, you have to whip up a batch of muffins. When you want to go to bed early, you can't because you have to wait for those muffins to finish baking.

With any measure of success, you will inevitably run into some constraints, either on time, storage, or level of commitment. It's a math equation that is rarely in your favor.

> *In the beginning, we started in our condo. We did everything out of our kitchen and our bedroom was the shipping room. Then our business exploded after hundreds of trials. We were working from 5 AM to 10 PM every day. My floors were shiny with cocoa butter. I got tendinitis in both my wrists from rolling out our squares. It was just too much. Fifteen thousand bars made by hand and I was getting close to a breakdown, so we knew we needed to find a place. We had to scale.*
> **—Lezlie Karls-Saltarelli, cofounder of Mid-Day Squares**

All that said . . .

As your business continues to grow, you will not be able to sustain it out of your home. You know you aren't going to be able to get a retail account because working from your home doesn't give you the insurance, licenses, and the food-grade certifications you'll need. If you get a meaningful buyer, they're going to want to see that documentation. You sense that you will have to move to some sort of shared kitchen or commercial contract manufacturer at some point. Do you want to call it quits now and say, "Hey, it was fun while it lasted," or push on and find a shared kitchen?

Decision: Do you quit or find a shared kitchen?

To **quit**, turn to page 31

To **find a shared kitchen**, turn to page 33

There isn't any shame in stopping while you're ahead. This is actually quite common, particularly in the farmers' market world. Turnover is high. Typically, a business doesn't stay in the farmers' market circuit for more than two or three months. Nina Jolic, cofounder of enci sweets, experienced this firsthand.

CASE STUDY

Nina Jolic

I 've wanted to sell my gluten-free, dairy-free cookies since I moved to Encinitas, California, six years ago when I saw how popular farmers' markets were in the area. I felt farmers' markets would allow me the opportunity to try the concept before deciding if it was the right type of business for me.

In the beginning, you have to do it all by hand. I was spending fourteen hours in the kitchen baking, and I knew from a previous food business that waste is a problem in the food industry, so I was weighing each cookie to make sure they were the same size. I didn't have a machine to do that for me.

Then I went to the farmers' market from 10 AM to 2 PM every weekend, plus setup and takedown, so it was another five hours of time. And as you know, time is money. On slow days, I may only have had $250 in gross sales. This didn't cover the overhead or cost of my time, which is often the case when you start a business. You don't get paid for your time.

I started analyzing the sales numbers, time and effort, overhead costs, and future revenue projections and associated expenses. To grow the business, I couldn't possibly do it all myself so that would mean hiring to produce more cookies to drive revenue growth. I could see that it would take three to five years to earn the income that I needed if I was doing this full time. I was not willing to quit my job to do this the right way, and doing it as a side hustle made no financial sense, nor was it good for me personally to be working seven days a week. If I had done this analysis at the start, I probably never would have got into the farmers' market, but I wanted to also gauge how the physical labor would affect my viewpoint on doing this business.

After two months at the farmers' markets, I decided my vision required too much sacrifice and at this stage of my life, with a daughter to support in college, made it not viable. I have no regrets, though. It was a fun adventure and I'm an adventurous person. It was something I had always wanted to do, and I'm so happy I did it. Otherwise I would have wondered if the business was viable!

THE
END

Because continuing to work from home no longer works for you, you have to go to a shared kitchen. Shared kitchens can be great.

Shared kitchens are popping up more and more. Sometimes they're called commercial kitchens. They are food-grade facilities where you can rent time. There are bunches of them in most communities. Finding them is as easy as an internet search.

Think of them kind of like a coworking space but for food producers. They usually have a lot of the equipment you will need, the sort of things you would have to buy on your own if you were doing it at home. So that's a bonus. They also have specialized equipment you wouldn't have, like the machines needed to put your product on a pallet and then wrap that pallet, for example. They will also have the licenses, permits, insurance, and other benefits you likely don't have at home.

It is a little more complicated now, though, because you have to go buy your ingredients from the three stores and the online vendor to arrive at the same time, then you have to store those ingredients until you can transport them to the kitchen or buy storage space.

You also have to schedule time. You have to find blocks where you can reserve the space fitting your own time and that of the people you are using to help you, and then make sure all your ingredients are delivered by then. If everything doesn't fall into place, you burn your hours and you can't produce. Ingredients start to spoil.

Once you are there, you have to be efficient with your time. You probably want a couple of people so you can get a little assembly line going. Usually you use friends and family at this stage. But here's the thing: friends and family only last so long as free labor. It's great for the first week or so, but then people get tired because they have lives to live.

If you want storage space to leave your ingredients, you can rent that, but it's an added cost. Everything is by the hour. If you only use certain equipment, you pay for that along with a cleaning fee in most cases.

Now remember, you have a free-from item. It can be really hard to maintain that in a shared kitchen because other people are using things that have allergens, and you can't guarantee everything is getting a deep clean before you come in. So yes, you might find a commercial kitchen, but you might not be able to label your muffins "free from" anymore. You'll see on bags: "processed in a facility that also processes dairy and nuts" and similar warnings. If there is any chance that such substances are processed in that shared kitchen, you may have to add such a label to your muffin packaging to indicate potential cross contamination. Suddenly your "free from" muffins are no longer guaranteed to be free from those substances.

So then you think maybe you'll just bring in your own specialized, clean equipment. Some shared kitchens allow that and some don't—that's a gamble.

And now your product is not meeting your standards. Some people might suggest you just go find a big, allergen-free co-packer or even build your own facility. But remember, that's not Angela's purpose. She doesn't want her path to lead to a massive commercial enterprise. This is a small thing that she does because of the passion. But you have to do something.

All that said . . .

Thank your lucky stars! Somehow you are able to find a shared kitchen that works for you with the standards you need to keep. Hooray!

Day one, you book time, you're in the shared kitchen, you've got the equipment. You've gone to the grocery store. You bought all your ingredients. You have a friend who you suckered into helping you. Time to get started. And maybe it takes four hours, maybe it takes eight hours. Depends. We've already gone over the fact that you have to gather everything beforehand and get on a schedule to make sure you optimize your time. Often, the tension faced by founders who opt for the shared kitchen arrangement boils down to cost versus quality.

Your problem now is that you have to justify the expense of that shared kitchen and the bulk ingredients you just bought. There are two looming questions you face:

1. How do you price your muffins?
2. Who is going to buy your muffins outside of friends and family?

In real life, these decisions are usually made simultaneously, but since we can't ask you to read two pages at the same time, let's start with price. Deciding where to sell the muffins will come soon.

Given your background in project management and business, you have tracked what your costs are so far. You have to decide how much you should charge to make all of this worth your time. You can price your product for profit or at a comparable rate to other muffins on the market.

Decision: Do you price your product at a comparable rate or price for profit?

To **price comparably**, turn to page 37

To **price for profit**, turn to page 39

You Price Comparably

Let's say you have already found a place to sell your muffins. You really want people to try your muffins without hesitating on price. You do some research and find out that most single-serve baked items on the market are between two and four dollars.

It costs you three dollars to make your muffins now because you're in the shared kitchen. The thinking goes like this: "Hey, if I want people to start trying what I am selling, they're going to hesitate over paying too much for a muffin. However, if I can sell more muffins, I can get my cost lower. If I can get my cost down to two dollars and then sell it for three dollars, that would be good."

And in some ways, you can get your costs down. You can buy bulk volume ingredients. You can find some efficiencies in the process, like doing bigger production runs. When you order packaging materials in bulk, costs go lower the bigger you get. It stands to reason that if you can sell more, you can charge less. So you decide to charge three dollars for a muffin that currently costs you about three dollars to make.

But this is where we need to talk about margins. You have to pay for the rental and the ingredients, sure. You factored that in. What you forgot is your time. People always forget to calculate their time.

How much is your time worth? Remember you had to spend time formulating the recipe, buying ingredients, scheduling, making the batter, waiting for it to bake, and the actual time it takes to sell them. It all adds up.

When you add in your time, it turns out you've been working for pennies. So you decide to raise your price so you can make a profit.

But you can't! You can't suddenly raise the price more than two times what it was. Who is going to pay five dollars for a muffin that only cost them three dollars last week? So now you're feeling depressed.

All that said . . .

You can't achieve the scale because you are losing money, so your options are to quit because it's not worth it or to start raising money for marketing and branding so you can sell more. In this industry, this phase is about selling the "sizzle" more than the steak. You have to really make it special, and to do that, you need money. You can always go to friends and family and see if they will help you raise money for marketing.

Decision: Do you quit or go to friends and family?

To **quit**, turn to page 31

To **go to friends and family**, turn to page 55

I'm frequently told that people like Pass the Honey's honeycomb, but it is too expensive. The price is the price it has to be right now at our size. If we were to lower it even a dollar, we would be in negative territory, unable to achieve the purpose we set out to achieve. Educating the consumer is a difficult path—it's costly and takes time, but I have to get comfortable with selling less than I'd like to get where I want to go. The product can't be priced lower than what you need to make your business work.

In this storyline, it costs you three dollars to make your muffins because you're in the shared kitchen. You're going to price it for profit, so you set it at five dollars a muffin. But you know this is a little high for what most people would comfortably pay for a muffin.

Nina Jolic, cofounder of enci sweets says, "At the farmers' market, because your product is handcrafted, buyers are aware, and you can sell for a higher price than a grocery store. Don't undersell. I sold my cookies for $3.75 and my partner sold her keto-donuts for six dollars each. And people were paying that!"

Now this is where we have to get into what it means to educate the consumer. You need to find a way to get face-to-face time so that you can convey the value of your muffins and explain what makes them special. If you're going to charge a higher price for something, people have to understand why they would want to pay that price. Essentially, your customers have to validate their own rationale as to why they're going to pay five dollars to you when they could buy a muffin for two dollars somewhere else. Or even three dollars somewhere else. If you are charging nearly twice what your competitors charge, people want to know why. It is done all the time, but it takes just that . . . time and money.

All that said . . .

You are fortunate enough to live in a community with an active farmers' market scene, and you have noticed that you are always willing to spend more money on food when you go to those markets. You have a sense a farmers' market is a good place to start selling your muffins.

And as a bonus, the most natural and easiest accessible place to get that face-to-face time you need is at a farmers' market. This aligns with Angela's decision to stay small and flexible.

To **go to a farmers' market**, turn to page 41

Farmers' markets are typically where most founders who start a home-based food business will end up. This is for a number of reasons, usually beginning with the desire to get immediate consumer feedback.

You don't mind spending a whole Saturday engaging with your community. It gives you a chance to meet other makers, get real-world feedback, and try out new things. It is a real high-touch sales environment. When a founder talks about their product, people purchase it because they like the story and they like supporting an individual over a faceless brand.

All that happens in real time, week in, week out at farmers' markets. So in a way, there is no better place to start understanding your customer and tinkering with your product. With that immediate feedback, you know what doesn't work, and you can innovate. Your batches are small so you don't have all that much invested yet, which means you can be versatile and nimble.

One thing you need to consider is that, depending on where you live, there could be a waiting list to get a spot. San Diego has fifty-two farmers' markets. New York City has fifty. There's always a waiting list for the best ones. They don't want conflicting vendors, so if there's another muffin person, you are not going to get in there until the other muffin people leave.

To get in, you meet with the farmers' market managers and determine if there's even an area for you to sell. Then they look at who else is there and make the determination. It could be weeks before you actually get booth space. It could even be months for an opening to become available in some of the best markets.

Then you have to make sure you have some money available. Sometimes you can rent the space for a flat rate or they'll take a percentage of profits. It works both ways—and sometimes there will be a minimal space fee and also a percentage. You need to buy a tent, a table, an apron, and any display materials. It's not a ton, of course. It can be as little as $100 but can get up to $1,000 pretty quickly. It's an investment all the same.

So now you've got these expenses on top of the costs of the commercial kitchen. Not to mention that you've got a perishable item, so there's some sense of urgency. You may end up having to travel and investing a lot of time trying to find a farmers' market nearby. You may have to start at a subpar market or one that is a long drive away. So that adds to your expenses: you need a vehicle that fits your table and displays, and you need to figure in the cost of fuel. And, as mentioned earlier, let's not forget the indirect cost of your time as you manage your booth and perhaps drive to distant locations. But that's what people do, so you bite the bullet and do it. Nina Jolic went down to the farmers' market.

CASE STUDY

Nina Jolic

When you go to the farmers' market, the customers are loyal. They do want to see that you're going to be there so they may wait three or four visits before they buy from you. The first time they see you, they may be curious, but they may just walk by. The second time they see you, they might come and try a sample. Your samples do not need to be big. They can be bite-size, the size of a quarter. The third time, they will maybe try and buy. Once they buy your products and like it, then many become loyal. Then you start to see them every week.

The thing about the farmers' market is that they are not all equal. Some are a waste of time because they don't have a big enough or consistent enough customer base. They may have a lot of browsers, touristy people, or people that are just out for a walk. Not buyers. The best ones are those that have customers that shop local.

Make sure you know which farmers' markets are the most lucrative. One person next to me in the farmers' market made about a thousand dollars a day with only one or two products and at another market made sixteen hundred dollars every week.

All that said . . .

Well done. You've had some measure of success selling your muffins— enough to make a nice little profit. Now you're faced with another decision. Would you like to continue to grow, or do you want to stop where you're at with your one little farmers' market and be happy that you've got enough incremental income to give you some profit?

Decision: Do you settle or grow?

To **settle**, turn to page 44

To **grow**, turn to page 47

You Settle

You have a small farmers' market business and a locally known name.

The good thing with creating a farmers' market–based business centered in your own community is that you actually get to enjoy life and take opportunities when you feel like you want to take them. Nothing is forced on you. If you want to take a few weeks off, you can. If you want to roll up the tent for a year, you can. You have everything in place to be able to proceed for the rest of your life making your muffins and bringing in a few thousand dollars every week, perhaps more.

Christopher Hesse, founder of Vukoo Nutrition said, "Until you get the OK to place your product in a retailer, farmers' markets are the way to go. In many places, they are killing it. Some are bringing in $5,000 to $10,000 a day on a weekend. Sample tables get immediate feedback."

All that said . . .

Most founders I have talked to can last about nine to twelve months in a farmers' market setting. If they don't grow anywhere, they get burned-out. It gets tedious giving up every weekend, and friends and family will usually only stick around for so long as volunteers, so you end up with higher costs to hire someone else. For the most part, if you pick farmers' markets, it's a fairly short-term run. I can only think of two brands that I know of that took the farmers' market route to retail and succeeded. It took ten years for each. Personally, I don't have that level of patience.

You've made the decision you're going to stay the course. You don't want to raise more funds. You don't want to push this thing to the moon. Don't let other people tell you that's a bad decision, or you should be doing this. The shoulds, the shoulds, the shoulds. Ugh.

You told yourself in the beginning, "This is what I want, this is how I'm measuring success," and you've gotten there. And you do not have the desire to push this thing to take on a global conglomerate. You're not trying to be an internationally known brand or founder. You're completely OK with having a meaningful amount of scale because you're supporting your life. You're benefiting your community. It's an honorable position to be in. There are thousands and thousands of such businesses; in fact, the lion's share of them in America are this type.

I think it's incredibly irrational that the expectation is that all businesses should grow infinitely. Nothing grows infinitely. It's an incredibly self-aware and disciplined thing to understand where your homeostasis lies. Everyone has different goals. If you've reached those goals, big kudos to you. You've done what you've set out to do, and you're living your life on your terms.

Growth is tough. It typically comes down to cash. You'll see that this tension underlies the entire book. Are you going to stay profitable by sacrificing growth? Or are you growing and sacrificing profitability? That tends to always be the constant struggle in the CPG business.

Once you accept money from other people, your company begins to take on a life of its own. Angela has the greatest chances of success because she gets to define what "success" is from the beginning of her journey and throughout the entire experience. She doesn't have to do anything she doesn't want to do.

Sure, everyone gets the itch when things are going well and money is coming in. You think, "I wonder if I could take this national?!" But in this story, you'll note that the more conservative choices were the ones that provided the most flexibility and freedom. When you don't extend yourself into risk too much, you retain your freedom.

But too often, somebody will come knocking and want your product. It's hard not to think, "That's interesting and fun. Let's give it a go." Then you try to ride the line, just going hand to mouth. There is a great deal of stress involved in that route, as you'll see with the other characters.

THE
END

If you'd like to grow, then you have another quick decision to make.

> **Decision:** Do you want to go into retail or do you want to expand by growing into more farmers' markets?
>
> To **go into retail**, turn to page 48
>
> To **go into more farmers' markets**, turn to page 57

You Go into Retail

This seems like the rational decision, right? But it's far more complicated than you might expect.

> There were other companies in our area who chose the farmers' market route. We didn't do that because we felt like it gives you a false sense of reality. Customers show up at farmers' markets to discover new things, but that doesn't mean it will translate into a massive market in the grocery store for your product. You will feel the love hard at a farmers' market and get punched in the face hard when you get to the grocery store.
>
> **—Nick Saltarelli, cofounder of Mid-Day Squares**

So let's talk about retail. If you decide to go into retail, you are now locked into the commercial kitchen. You are past the point of no return in that respect since you can't legally make your muffins from home because of licensing and insurance and all of that.

Most often when founders go into retail, they do it slowly. Every community has a local grocery store, cafés, restaurants, coffee shops, and those sorts of places. You make a list of every place you can think of where you can buy other muffins. You begin hitting the pavement to see if you can get in.

It's key that you take every meeting with every buyer. Don't farm out the actual engagement with a customer, be it the direct customer at a farmers' market or a direct buyer at a major retailer. That founder connection is critical. They need to see the "why" behind the reason your company exists. A lot of founders will hand that off to a salesperson a little earlier than they should, and the passion of the company is lost in that quick handoff. Plus, as a founder, it's very, very beneficial to sit with a buyer, hear any objections, and ask clarifying questions to understand and refine the pitch.

As a result of all this hard work, a buyer comes to you and says, "Hey, we'd like to sell these in our café. Can we buy wholesale from you?"

Great news! You're super excited. But you don't really know what the wholesale price is on homemade muffins. Because you marked your muffin at five dollars, the buyer will expect your wholesale price to be half that—$2.50. But don't forget that it still costs you three dollars to make them, and that's without your time.

You can see how margins and pricing interact to support or sink a business. But let's say that since this is a local business as well, and they believe in your mission, they are willing to give you a break and take less of a profit. A lot of retailers do that to help a new, local business get started.

It's a relief to realize you can still make a little profit. This gives you enough to actually buy the next round of ingredients for that next batch of muffins. You have enough profit to actually make a brand and to set up a website to promote it.

Everything goes along smoothly until word gets out and you get your first big retail order. A regional grocery chain wants to pick you up. It's a decent-size order and the numbers actually pencil out. You are fairly confident you can deliver. In fact you're getting pretty excited. You are going to make $2,000 for an order of muffins. It might have taken you ten farmers' markets to do that!

But once the shine wears off, you're scrambling. You begin to think through the ingredients you need and add up how much that will be. You have to figure out how to get it all delivered on the right date and reserve more time at your shared kitchen. Now you can certainly justify buying in bulk, which actually helps your cost a little bit. You're going to have to store it at the shared kitchen, so that's an added expense. You might have to hire a part-time person to help you manufacture because not many friends want to sit on a production line for free.

So the $2,000 is getting whittled down pretty quick. And to make matters worse, you learn you aren't going to see the payment for at least forty-five days. You hope you have the cash available to produce the goods and cover your overhead while waiting to get paid.

All that said . . .

You still have the next farmers' market, so you start running into cash-flow issues. This just means you are waiting for payment on goods you've already sent. You fronted the costs and are waiting to get the return.

While you wait, you still have a business to run that continues to consume cash. You can't keep this up for long, so you have a decision to make. There are three options available to you:

1. Go to friends and family and ask for investments to help you get by in exchange for a small ownership percentage.
2. Dip into your own savings.
3. Find a loan.

Decision: Do you try to find a loan, dip into your savings, or go to friends and family?

To **try to find a loan**, turn to page 52

To **dip into your own savings**, turn to page 53

To **go to friends and family**, turn to page 55

You Try to Find a Loan

You go to banks with no success.

Any lender is going to want a track record of at least two years, so you haven't been in business long enough. You're too young, too volatile, too small.

On top of that, they're going to want some sort of stability in the company. This means they want collateral before they will lend you the cash. You can mortgage your home, if you own one and have reasonable equity. But remember this was a side project. Do you really want to risk homelessness for your muffins?

Of course, some people might qualify for loans at this stage if they have revenue, collateral, and a product that bankers will get behind. There are all kinds of other nuanced lending, but for the lion's share, you need a strong track record, no preexisting debt, and collateral.

All that said . . .

You are denied.

Most people will say, "You don't want to stop the order. Just use your savings."

But that only lasts so long.

I can't even count how many times I have had to consider and actually act upon transferring the remainder of my savings into one of my companies. Even getting debt on one company to lend to another. It's nerve-wracking. You feel like you're stealing from Peter to pay Paul half the time, and at the end of the day, thank goodness in my case, I haven't had to live under a bridge. I have had to eat dog food before (just once!). You're essentially running a company on ramen and duct tape, and it's not fun.

You're probably starting to sense, in a consumer-goods business, cash flow and production of goods for inventory is a major constraint on growth. You can maybe cover this order, but then the retailer doubles the order the next month, and they haven't paid you yet.

After all the work you've done, you're really committed. Because you are in stores now, you want to ensure you make the very best product with the best packaging you can afford. Unfortunately, there's no money left for marketing or sales. You try really hard to make a run of it using only your own money and end up spending everything you have.

When you use your savings, you deplete your own disposable cash. In Angela's case, this can only last three or four cycles, if that. What if another retailer wants to come in? What do you do? The further you get down the line, the less expendable cash you have, and the closer your savings inches toward that scary zero.

You bought in bulk. Where are you going to store all that stuff? There are perishability concerns. Are you making one big run with everything—baking it all at one time and using up all the ingredients you purchased? Do you have leftovers? Or do you try to do it in two or three runs? What is the shelf life of the raw ingredients? What does not last on the shelf? Perishability and spoilage is a major concern on a massive production level. Now, when this is coming out of your own pocket, and you're sometimes having to pay retail prices for all the ingredients, it becomes a financial hindrance.

All that said . . .

You see the writing on the wall and you have to shut it down because there's no other way to get out. You're all out of money.

THE
END

You go to friends and family to raise funding. You even hit up your current customers to help you raise the money you need, and they support you.

This small group is usually made up of those people who always believed in you. With their help, you're able to fulfill the new accounts. When you are taking investment from your brother or your parents or your customers, this usually means you give away equity. But much like partnership documentation, do you have a structure to keep track of those sorts of deals?

"Friends and family" is a generic term, but it just means anyone who doesn't invest in your company professionally. They can be from anywhere. I'm pleasantly surprised and consistently shocked where checks come from and their size. I didn't believe I had any sort of investors in my friends and family or even general acquaintances when I began my business.

I don't have rich friends and family, but they don't need to be rich. Your job isn't to judge what they may or may not be able to do. Your job is to be passionate about what you do and share that passion. When you start talking about things you're doing, especially if they are interesting, support materializes. I have been surprised at the decent-size checks I get from people in my coworking environment when they learn what I do. One young man who also shares the space came over one day and asked me what I did, and we got to talking. That afternoon he found me again and handed me a very good-size check. At the time, it was my company's biggest check to date.

The largest investor in Pass the Honey is someone I have never met in person. We connected through another person I have never met.

This investor's checks started small, and when he liked what we were doing and how I communicated, his checks kept coming and getting bigger. Every time I send out an email, he sends more funding. He is our number one investor and that number one fan and really likes what we're doing. He's not even in the food space. He reads my emails and has great feedback and questions for me all the time. Obviously I give him as much attention as I can, and I am so grateful for the value and ideas he brings to the table. More so than any professional investor I've ever worked with.

All that said . . .

Your name starts to spread, and you get more accounts. Now it's time to decide if you want to grow regionally by expanding into more farmers' markets or raise the money from professional investors that you will need to grow nationally.

Decision: Do you expand into other farmers' markets or do you want to raise funds from professional investors?

To **go into more farmers' markets**, turn to page 57

To **raise funds from professional investors**, turn to page 134

This is a nice choice. This means less stress in the long run. You kind of take on what you can when you can. It can become a lovely little cash-flowing business if you want it to.

Once you decide to expand into more farmers' markets, you have to hire more staff because, obviously, you can't be in more than one place at a time. This means you have to educate the new staff, and then you have to trust that even though you, the founder, are not there talking about it, the product will be marketed well.

Because you're selling a high-dollar muffin, you've got to find the right staff who share your passion. They need to know all the nuances, and that takes time. And it takes continuity. The concern now is that if your sales aren't meeting your expectations, you wonder if it's because the new market location doesn't work or because the product is not being conveyed properly.

You might have to be in five farmers' markets for five months to break even, which means five (or even ten) more tables, tents, aprons. It's more of everything. And you might not see the return on that investment for a while. At least until repeat customers come back and you get your dedicated clientele at that market.

First you need to understand what works at one market, and then multiply that by multiple markets on the same day, which will obviously either double or quadruple or quintuple your production demands for the previous week at whatever facility you're producing your goods.

You're not just replicating yourself. You're replicating the infrastructure, and you're trying to replicate it in a way that is consistent with establishing a branding effort. Even at the early stages, you want to start delivering on that brand and that promise, and not just the quality of the goods but the entire experience. This is called scaling.

Can you afford really high-quality staff or are you just using friends? How long are those friends going to stick around and be there every weekend? Are you paying them super well? Are they trustworthy? Remember they are handling cash. Are you training these folks? Are you creating a long-term business? Are they really representing the business? Can they speak to the depths of the brand and the product like you can? Are you just trying to fill space with bodies? There are a lot more moving parts now.

In the meantime, you're depleting your savings or you're borrowing money from friends or giving up equity in your company for investors. That's tough.

Once you're in business for two years, you hit that magic number. You qualify for loans at that point, which means you could grow more in a couple of years if you wanted to. But for now, you settle in for a nice long duration at your farmers' markets.

All that said . . .

Way to go!

You did exactly what you set out to do. You have a nice little business that brings in some extra spending money.

In fact, you were able to get to a point where money is not a considerable constraint anymore. You maybe have a six-figure income, if you're lucky. You are able to send your children to college and even take a few nice vacations in the off-season from the farmers' markets. And in the end, you are satisfied that you shared your free-from muffins with the people in your community. You showed restraint and because of that, you can enjoy the rest of your life.

If you want to be a nomad and live as free as a bird, you can more or less do what you want at last. You've written your own destiny, and for that, I commend you.

THE
END

Nathaniel's PATH

You Are Now Nathaniel

You have to keep your day job and support yourself outside the business. You want to try to do as much as you can on your own, particularly when it comes to funding, but you realize that there will probably come a point when that won't work anymore. You just hope to go solo as long as you can.

You truly believe your energy drink, ExtraMetaNomNom, could upend the soda business because it's actually good for you. It's just as refreshing as soda, and it fulfills the craving for sweetness. Essentially, it does everything that soda was doing for you, and you have no doubt it will satisfy any customer who tries it.

You are creative, passionate, and ready to go. But you don't know what you are doing. The first thing you need to decide is if you are going to teach yourself how to run a beverage business, or if you're going to hire experts to teach you.

A dream is great, but it doesn't give you knowledge or experience. You are faced with researching the endless depths of the internet to find information on formulation, on packaging, or even making your product on a scale beyond throwing ingredients in a blender at home. Do you want to continue trying to figure it out on your own, or do you feel it would be worthwhile to pay an expert to advise you?

Decision: Do you do it yourself or hire an expert?

To **do it yourself**, turn to page 63

To **hire an expert**, turn to page 66

You are a scrapper, aren't you? When choosing the "do it yourself" route, you are literally starting from square one, which means it's going to take you a lot longer to learn what to do.

You got this. Between master-class seminars and all the knowledge that's at your fingertips and on the internet, you feel like you can master any part of the company. This means you're going to beef up your knowledge of the industry. Remember, though, you're a savvy marketer. You know the internet. You know there's knowledge out there. You are well connected through your family and peer groups.

But you don't know the terms. You don't know the rules. You don't have relationships with manufacturers or distributors or retailers. You spend every spare minute on the internet and sending emails, following every rabbit trail for every question you can think of.

When you really start to get into this industry, just like any industry, it might look easy on the outside to someone who has never done it. You know how to make a product and sell a product, but you don't know the complexities behind everything. The process becomes very nuanced, and there's specific language you have to learn. There are regulations you have to be aware of. There are countless industry groups. Understanding all the intricacies takes time and patience.

The key question here is: Where do you begin? Is it operations? Is it finance? Is it marketing? Is it branding? Is it the technical aspects of producing content on websites and social media and learning to implement "click funnels" and "ad extensions"? Is it sales, bookkeeping, and taxes? Which is the element that will give you the best advantage for the next phase of your growth?

Understanding where the tension of the company is will be crucial at all stages of growth. You'll ask about the constraints, bottlenecks, and where you should allocate your time. It will take you a while to learn new tasks, new skills, and new categories of the business operations.

You ask around and see who in your circles knows someone who has a food company or who's worked for bigger companies. You start asking a lot of questions and buying a lot of coffees for other people. You have a lot of conversations, and from those, you collect many opinions that you have to sift through. Eventually you start to get an idea of what some of your paths and decisions may entail.

All of this can take a long time, and patience is not something you have. You want to build your brand quickly and make it as big as possible. You get overwhelmed and confused quickly.

You are starting to get exasperated because you feel like the market is primed. This is the time for your product to come out. No other time has been so focused on healthy food as it is right now. You feel like you're moving through molasses.

You get frustrated. You keep asking yourself, "Will I ever understand everything there is to know about food? Maybe I'm not cut out for this at all."

You start to wonder if maybe this isn't the best idea. There is too much to learn, and you're overwhelmed. You remain passionate about your recipe and the mission of the company, but you still have to hold down your day job.

You really want to be like Christopher Hesse, founder of Vukoo Nutrition, when he said, "I just want to see how far I can take it!"

All that said . . .

After considering your options and the effort you have put in so far with no progress, you decide it's too much. You give up before you even begin.

Enjoy your recipe. Share it with your friends and family. It becomes just something you do that people know about. And your life is good . . . enough.

You Hire an Expert

With this decision, you recognize that you are spending money on something that's not going to return anything. At least not for a bit. But you do it anyway because you know it will save you a lot of time. And isn't time money?

You have so many questions. Do you launch a website before you have a product? Where do you find sourcing groups and manufacturers? Who should you hire to design your packaging? Should you do pre-sales while you are focusing on formulation and ingredients? All of this can be very overwhelming, and you need help.

You find an expert by asking family, friends, friends of friends, everyone you can think of. You join industry associations to make contacts. You find somebody who's worked for big companies before, perhaps for a retailer or in a restaurant setting, really anything in the food and beverage industry.

Once you locate your expert, you will either pay them a retainer or agree to equity. Sometimes you pay a flat fee, but no matter how you look at it, you're spending money for advice, not for work. You're buying strategy and insights, not actionable execution.

The expert will give you guidance and you will take careful notes. At this stage, you are a blank slate, so you listen to everything they say. If you've hired the right advisor, they not only will give you a global, macro view of what's going on, they'll also give you the pros and cons of the decisions you have to make. They'll guide you in directions that should have the least impact or the least financial costs involved.

One of the most important benefits they offer is to make introductions. If you have a really good expert, they'll introduce you to plenty of other founders and other formulators who can give you tips. They will connect you to other groups they've worked with in the past. It's kind of like getting a cofounder without having a cofounder.

You still have to make all the tough decisions. Ultimately you are the only one who will have all the intelligence, but at least now you're making more educated decisions.

All that said . . .

You work with this expert for a while. You appreciate their consultations, but at some point you have to cut them loose. They've made the introductions. They've given you advice to get to the next step, and now paying a monthly retainer for the occasional meeting doesn't make financial sense anymore.

You kindly say, "Thank you for your good advice," and send them on their way.

In my case, I spent $280,000 on an expert that botched a product launch and cost the company more than $700,000 in lost revenue because they didn't cross their t's and dot their i's and refused to admit their mistake, even in the face of hard evidence through a third party. Then they tried to come after me for the remainder of their contract, which I politely declined. I don't know if this is common or uncommon, but it was really painful for a new company; I had deferred to him before I knew what I was doing. I just didn't know enough to hold anyone accountable, and I got burned.

Let's say something similar happens to you. Now you have a smaller budget than you started with, but you have a better idea of how to get where you want to go. Do you continue to self-fund and devote what money you have left toward branding and marketing to create demand, or do you put it into developing your product so you have a supply to sell?

Decision: Do you invest in creating demand (marketing) or in your product (supply)?

To **invest in marketing**, turn to page 69

To **invest in supply**, turn to page 78

When you market a product that hasn't yet been made, you run the risk of "fake it till you make it" syndrome.

You've chosen to invest in marketing to create the demand for the product. If you generate a ton of consumer interest, you know you're going to be stuck trying to expand your production, but that's a risk you're willing to take. The goal is to make sure everything looks legitimate. Expenses in marketing include branding, logo, packaging, and comps. Everything is about generating interest in the product.

The key to success was our online sample program. We sold samples on our website at fifty cents a pack. We asked people for credit cards to ensure they were committed to the bar that way. Then we spent a ton of time making custom Polaroid pictures and handwritten notes that we placed inside the packages, on top of the bars. We'd research the person who ordered the bar and take a Polaroid we knew would resonate with them. Then we hand delivered the bar. This really drove virality. People opened their bars and saw the photos and were freaking out that we did that. Every time we did this, we increased our presence. They'd get the bar and then see us making the bars on social media. It's OK to do things that are not scalable at the beginning. Of course, we knew it wasn't scalable. But it was OK! You figure it out as you go.

—Lezlie Karls-Saltarelli, cofounder of Mid-Day Squares

When you invest in a great website, it becomes real to people. Sometimes it actually helps you raise money. There is a perceived value and perception of reality. You can have a very small company that presents very large on the internet.

On the flip side, if you have this great presence and people think the product is available but it's not (because you haven't made it yet), you run the risk of turning off your customers because there's a lag in the orders. They'll wonder, "Why am I even on this website when there's nothing available to buy?" or "Where the heck is my order?"

Some people invest a great deal in giving away free product to influencers. They justify this because they think if they can get positive exposure with the right people, it will lead to greater sales down the line. This rarely moves the needle. One specific social media post from certain celebrities might move the needle. But most of the time, you need multiple continuous posts to reinforce it. How dedicated are influencers going to be to your product?

> *I've heard from others' experiences that celebrities can come to the table and just want to get equity for service. For many, this rarely works out. For us, we were fortunate to have a celebrity come on board who was one of those perfect cultural fits for our company. Our personalities meshed really well, and we shared the same vision.*
>
> *In my observation, though, investing in influencers and celebrities just doesn't move the needle as much as you'd think, unless they are very strategically chosen. The celebrity will end up with a significant amount of equity, and the founder ends up left with a disappointing amount in the end because the celebrity didn't move the dial as expected on the business, in terms of sales and revenue.*
>
> **—Cassandra Curtis, cofounder of Once Upon a Farm**

The general rule is five touches. Typically, you need to reach the new consumer five times before they are moved to buy. This is incredibly costly. The idea of creating demand first rarely works.

And if it works, you're kind of behind the eight ball to produce. So this just kind of takes you back to having a product close to ready or ready to launch.

The biggest problem through all of this is that you're going to be spending a lot of money while not being able to generate income. It's a delicate balance. You can't technically sell anything until you have something to sell. You work around that with tactics like inviting customers to join a waiting list and doing preorders. All of this gives you an idea of what the demand is. This can be valuable because when you go to a manufacturer, you'll understand how much volume you need.

All that said . . .

In most cases, when you choose to invest in marketing first, the product rarely ever takes off. You wind up having very low interest or even lower sales, perhaps a couple hundred sales, which defeats you. It makes you a little depressed because you expected hundreds of thousands. You feel bad because, to put it metaphorically, you thought your baby was cute but nobody else agrees.

But the catch is this: You're not putting all your effort into the marketing because you know you don't have a product to sell, so you're never really giving it a full chance. Because you can't go all in on marketing first, you're not going to see the full results. In a way, it's almost a fool's errand.

This leaves you with the choice to invest more money in marketing or to invest in supply, or well, that's it. Your idea just wasn't as good as you thought it was.

Decision: Do you invest more money in marketing, invest in supply, or give up?

To **invest more in marketing**, turn to page 73

To **invest in supply**, turn to page 78

To **give up**, turn to page 80

Investing in marketing can be a tricky thing.

In the beginning, we spent a lot of money (and time) on different websites. The brand has taken a lot of iterations to get to where we are right now. There's always going to be changes, but in the beginning, I think we put too much into funding digital partners that weren't right for us. It was kind of a nightmare. We've also spent a good amount on iterations of consumer research, which can be a good thing to minimize risk. However, I think some of the best consumer research you can do is to ask target consumers in your network what they think of it, gather some initial data, and then launch online to gather quick and real-time feedback. Sometimes what a consumer says in a survey is not indicative of how they will actually purchase online or at retail.

—Cassandra Curtis, cofounder of Once Upon a Farm

But regardless of the risks, you decide to pull out all the stops and keep on marketing. You generate interest by dumping everything you have into it. You go all in and actually catch a tiger by the tail. Seemingly overnight, there's a ton of interest.

But you still don't have product to sell. And now you're managing customer complaints about delays.

You have no choice. You have to focus on producing a product. You have to follow up on those promises you've been making. You're a young company with an unproven track record. You have not delivered a single product yet, so you are going to have to scrape together every penny you have and get your product out the door.

Mid-Day Squares is one of the most enlightened, self-aware, authentic, and soulful brands out there today. Cofounder Jake Karls explained one factor in their success.

> We invested a lot of time into learning the lifestyle of our customer at first. We'd find our customer and then learn about their route. We knew they went to certain coffee shops, the poke bowl place, the gym, specific clothing stores, etc. We stepped into their route digitally using social media, and then physically by placing our brand along their routes. Their life was followed by Mid-Day Squares everywhere they went. It was all about building brand awareness. We chose this on purpose. In fact, a midsized local chain came and wanted a contract and everyone said go with that, but our product wasn't ready. But that was our choice and it paid off in the end.
>
> **—Jake Karls, cofounder of Mid-Day Squares**

This seems as good a place as any to talk about packaging choices. A lot of times there are labeling requirements that maybe haven't been thought through. I've sat through one too many meetings where the address of the company was left off the label. That's a no-no. One founder actually told me that they used the last money to make those labels, so they had nothing left to fix that mistake.

If you don't follow the labeling requirements, a retailer can't sell your product. They're going to want UPCs, and there are some logistical hoops you'll have to jump through to be able to be slotted into a retail setting. Insurance, things of that nature.

But I want to put in a plug for the expense of a professional designer. I have known people who paid a few hundred or even a few thousand dollars to a friend who said, "I could totally design your package," only to find that since that friend didn't know the requirements or dimensions of retail, that money completely went to waste. There's also something to be said for a brand that looks very professional right out of the gate based solely on the packaging. The Mid-Day Squares team is a great example of this.

> One of the main things we decided right off the bat was that the product had to look like a national CPG right away to give credibility. We used all our resources for less than $2,500 to build high-quality, professional packaging design first, and we finalized formulation at the same time we were developing the packaging. We chose to do a 3,000-package run, knowing that it was going to be super expensive on a per-unit basis. But we'd rather spend a lot to hold little inventory than spend a little per unit but have to order over 100,000 packages. Cash flow was always our number one priority. As soon as our brand started bumping on social media, stores reached out thinking we were ready for national placement right away. As our volume scaled, we negotiated better pricing on all raw ingredients and materials. Don't get caught on the trap of ordering more inventory for lower prices early on. Pro tip: Make sure you actually have the volume!
>
> **—Nick Saltarelli, cofounder of Mid-Day Squares**

All that said . . .

You catch a lucky break and find that all the interest you generated led to some *investor* interest. You get just enough money to move your focus to supply. You better thank your lucky stars because this doesn't always happen. Most people at this stage still have a very hard time getting in front of investors because they're an unproven entity.

Now that your marketing push has paid off and you can shift your focus, you have to decide how you're going to actually produce your product. One option is to go with something called a co-packer. It's a professional company that does commercial-scale food production. A lot of times, you'll have to line up some of the inventory or the raw materials. Or the co-packer can purchase them—it depends. If you're looking for a potato chip, there are groups that do potato chips. Or if you're looking for an energy bar, there are groups that specialize in energy bars. The thing here is that you face much longer production schedules. They are a professional operation, and with that there are standards. It might take a little longer to find the right partner.

You can go with a small co-packer, a large co-packer, or you can build your own facility. From your research, you know a small co-packer will probably provide a greater level of flexibility and availability, but they are few and far between and often have a lot of problems because they don't have the means that a large co-packer does. If you go with one that's a little more mature and established, you may feel like you're getting nickeled and dimed. Everywhere you turn there's another cost, or a fee, or a delay. And you have to get everything packaged, or all your raw materials have to be delivered to the co-packer and stored first, before you get scheduled. But you can make changes on the fly. You don't have to build tons of inventory. You can kind of build it as you need it. Warehousing costs sometimes are negligible. Maybe they won't charge you for some, because they're grateful for the business.

A large co-packer, on the other hand, will probably have an efficient and streamlined process, but getting on the schedule as a new company can be impossible due to their larger contracts with bigger companies. Some people jump right to building their own facilities, which gives you ultimate control and all of the expense.

And again, it can be a complete nightmare. A lot of times that co-packer role is vital to a brand when they're just getting their legs under them. There's no perfect option. There's no one size fits all.

Decision: Do you go with a large co-packer, a small co-packer, or build your own facility?

To **go with a large co-packer**, turn to page 81

To **go with a small co-packer**, turn to page 85

To **build your own facility**, turn to page 97

You Invest in Supply

OK, so you're going to take your money and use most of it to develop your product. You believe that you need to have the product in hand before you can sell it.

You're a young company with an unproven track record. You have not delivered a single product yet, so this seems like the logical choice. You figure you can generate a measure of interest after production. But you seem to be having a very hard time getting investors to nibble because you're an unproven entity. You figure you can worry about that after you get all this delicious, nutritious product into a package and ready to go.

Investing in your supply includes research, travel, relationship building, trust building, negotiations, and touring of facilities. This can be a real time drain, but it has to be done.

You'll have to line up all the packaging beforehand as well. Sometimes it's just a bag and a sticker. Other times you want something a little more polished. Again, it depends on where you're taking this, if it's a farmers' market or if you're looking to sell into local coffee shops. The point here is you're trying to get a start.

Then you have to find ingredients that can be scarce because other brands are purchasing the same things in bulk. It can feel like a dogfight to get the quantity you need on the timeline you want. Multiply that by the number of ingredients you have and the coordination time to get everything at the same place at the same time without anything expiring, and you're looking at a logistical nightmare.

Keep in mind you are cash strapped because no sales means no income. In choosing not to market, you deplete your funds without generating any demand. You run the risk that once you have it, no one's going to buy it.

All that said . . .

You've made it. You've got a price. You've got your ingredients. You've made your first run. There is very little left over, but you stuck the landing. Even if you haven't stuck the landing, you're ready to sell your product.

Now you have a warehouse room full of pallets of your product, just sitting there, slowly expiring. You have forty-five days to move this or it all goes to the landfill.

This means you have no choice. You have to invest whatever money you can find into marketing so you can move this product.

To **invest in marketing**, turn to page 147

You Give Up

You gave it all you had. Better luck next time!

Enjoy your recipe. You certainly have had a fun ride and you've learned a lot in the process. Don't feel too bad: 98 percent of all start-ups end up the same way, so you're in good company.

As Christopher Hesse, founder of Vukoo Nutrition says, "Be aware and be wise and grow from where you are with what you have today. Don't beat yourself up. There's a reason why you did what you did."

THE END

You decide that you want to go with a big co-packer because you still believe your idea is awesome and so it's worth it.

Some founders don't want to use a co-packer that is working for competing brands. Here's the thing. Co-packers are going to be packing for your competitors. They are. I think it's a concern that is unwarranted most of the time, especially if you go with a professional operation. Not much in food is proprietary, so if you can out-market and have higher-quality goods than a competitor, do it. The fear that your competitors will pinch your recipes doesn't really happen. If you're truly worried about this, build your own facility. But since you just decided not to build your own facility, this is what you've got.

Working with a large co-packer that knows your category can be amazingly beneficial because you're just placing an order for finished goods. They can do everything that you need to get a finished product. They order and store the ingredients and packing materials. They coordinate the schedule and make sure everything runs smoothly. They actually produce the product, package it, store it, and ship it for you. Seasoned co-packers have long-term contracts, which means long-standing relationships with executives. They have specialized accounts and legal teams to help you through the process.

But the downside is you have minimum order quantities (MOQ), which are required order amounts you have to be ready to pay for.

This MOQ is usually the stumbling block for a lot of small start-ups. The co-packer may require you to order X number of bags or X

number of master cases, bars, beverages, whatever. They're going to ask for some volume because, again, they make their money on volume as they do for other competitors.

This is where you can go back to your expert if you hired one. Or you can do a lot of internet research. There are resources, but you have to know where to look. And these bigger co-packers have large contracts with big companies that will take precedence over your puny little operation. Most of them won't even respond to your call. It's going to be a while before you can even get your foot in the door.

Once you find a big co-packer, you have to make sure they have the right certifications, the right equipment, and the ability to buy the ingredients. If you have special ingredients or you have specialized packaging, that makes it more complicated.

Founders too often like to make these decisions in the beginning because they think it makes their product super unique, like having a special box size or some exotic and rare ingredient. Remember, rare ingredients are rare for a reason, and if they are hard to find, the co-packer may not want to mess with that and will insist on changing to something they can easily source. Similarly, a special box size doesn't fit on standard packaging equipment, and it may cause a lot of problems when it's on the shelves. Big co-packers won't want to get specialized machinery for your little order so that you can be in your special taller box or thinner bag or whatever. It's not worth the money to them. You'll have to compromise.

So the things founders do to separate their product from everything else on the market make the product more difficult to produce because it doesn't fit the traditional mold of what a contract manufacturing facility has available. It's one thing to get your customers' attention with something unique and novel, and it's another thing to be able to produce that unique and novel thing at volume. They weirder you get, the harder it is to produce.

At this stage, you're lucky to get the time of day from these places, so don't be a difficult client.

All that said . . .

You start to get discouraged, but you finally find a co-packer who has agreed to talk with you. You get excited for that call, but it's bad news. The co-packer then tells you about a competitor who has a brand similar to yours, who was not a competitor yesterday, but they are one today. And they're making a very similar product with this co-packer, and they have reserved the last available place on the production line. They have more money and they have bigger orders than you, so they get priority.

Dang it. You were so close.

So now your new choice is that you have to exceed the MOQ by placing a larger order than the competitor to knock them off the production schedule. Or you can move to a smaller co-packer. Or you bag it and you say, "I tried hard enough, but it's never going to work."

Ultimately, it's going to come down to what can you afford. Sometimes you can afford to go with a very large co-packer and spend the time preparing to start production. Other times, you end up getting anxious, or you have a finite window that you need to produce for a deadline.

Decision: Do you move to a small co-packer, commit to a larger order, or give up?

To **go with a small co-packer**, turn to page 85

To **commit to a larger order**, turn to page 89

To **give up**, turn to page 80

This is where you enter the world of compromises.

There are benefits to using a small co-packer because they're more flexible. They won't have the same big MOQs so you can do smaller runs, which is less of a risk if your product doesn't sell. But sometimes they are your only choice when you can't get on with a large co-packer and you don't have enough capital to build your own facility.

Small co-packers are even harder to find than big ones. You're going to call everyone in the industry you know—all of your friends and friends of your friends. I found the co-packer we use for Pass the Honey through our equipment manufacturer. They knew where another piece of equipment was that was like ours. So that was helpful. But much of it was luck. Total luck.

A lot of founders tell me they want their co-packer to be located in their city. This does not need to be the case. In fact, I would highly recommend you don't constrain yourself. You're going to want to find the best partner, that has the best equipment, that has the best timelines, and the MOQs that fit your needs. Every company I've been a part of has a co-packer that is not in the city it's been founded in, and it's worked out entirely fine. A lot of times it's centrally located because of fulfillment and shipping, so that's another consideration if you are on one of the coasts.

Small co-packers can sometimes be rinky-dink operations. They may or may not have the equipment you need, so you may or may not have to buy your own equipment. They sure as heck aren't going to be buying all your ingredients for you; they're going to make you buy all the ingredients. You have to coordinate how to get everything to the facility on their operation schedule. It's a lot more work. And there's a learning curve on both sides.

Additionally, there can be high turnover in staff, so there is some volatility in the way they work. They might've said they would warehouse your stuff for free, and then they'll charge you a pallet storage fee a month later.

When you make this decision, you have to look at the trade-offs and decide if it's worth it. You're not able to get continuity. You may not be getting professionalism. You're probably getting a lot more headache, but you don't have to order nearly as much material. It's way easier to get time on the production floor, and overall wait times are smaller. They don't have a ton of work. So you have a little bit more leverage when it comes to timing and matters of that nature.

I've been able to grow with smaller co-packers, but it wasn't without its problems. Sure there were mistakes, but at least we got a product to market. To me, that's the whole point: even if it was not perfect, I was OK. That devil of perfection will get you. One founder who knows this very well is Christopher Hesse, founder of Vukoo Nutrition.

CASE STUDY

Christopher Hesse

In January 2018, I had my first order for 20,000 units. This was going to be enough cases to get us growing like a real food business. I found a co-packer and placed my equipment. Then overnight they went bankrupt, locked the doors, and didn't even tell us. It took months to get another co-packer to fulfill that order.

I did a lot of tours and found a place that was really sketchy near where I lived. I could afford it and they had room for me, but ultimately, I said no because of the conditions. I always wanted to be transparent with my customers. I wanted to know that they could come see where our product was being made and that I would be fine with that.

I found another place in a different state that was super clean but small. It seemed to be a good stepping stone and I needed them. It turned out they were building an addition and their electrical system wasn't set up, so they were willing to build to my specs. After ten weeks, and $5,000 out of my pocket for a legal contract, the co-packer still hadn't set the facility up the way I needed.

Then once it was all set up, there was a delay on the tech side. They misprinted the film for my packaging. I had to reschedule that. Then paperboard got backed up four months for the rest of the packaging while they waited for enough orders to do bulk production.

Then the co-packer changed the terms. They came to me and said, "We can't front ingredients for you anymore." Certain key elements took us there in the first place, and now they're backtracking.

My advice when you're working with a co-packer is to get everything in writing and keep track of every draft. I've learned people won't sign a contract unless they know how to get out of it. You are money to them. They see you and they wonder if you're going to fail. Sometimes you have to show them what they said in the past. No matter how nice people are, they are still people, and they can screw you over, especially when it comes to business. Try to keep the emotion out and stay neutral. Good partnerships are hard to come by.

All that said . . .

You have a unique packaging design that you really think revolutionizes the customer experience with your product and you aren't willing to compromise, so you need a specialized piece of equipment. No surprise, this small co-packer does not have that equipment. So now you're faced with a new decision. Are you going to buy that piece of equipment yourself or are you going to commit to a large enough order that the co-packer will purchase it themself?

Decision: Do you commit to a larger order or buy equipment?

To **commit to a larger order**, turn to page 89

To **buy your own equipment**, turn to page 91

When you choose to go with a larger run, you choose to commit your finances to that. You have to be able to pay for that order.

It's all money, in this case. The co-packer is smaller, more nimble, and flexible. This means they are able to help you with creative solutions. The problem is they can't justify the expense of this piece of equipment that may only get used by you unless they have a guaranteed return on their investment. It has to be worth the effort.

If you commit to a certain volume of orders over a period of time, they'll buy the equipment and it'll pay itself off based on the orders that you're committing to. That helps save you some money, which you can put into marketing. So you do this; you commit to your future success.

Let's say you originally agreed to an MOQ for 20,000 units. Now they want you to double that for the equipment, so you're looking at 40,000 units.

But because this is a smaller co-packer, things are going to go awry pretty quickly. They say they can do it, but they've never done this big a run before. They order the machine, but there are shipping delays. Then once it comes, they have to get trained on how to use it, which takes time.

In fact, it takes forever. The ingredients don't show up all at the same time, so some begin to expire, and then when you get that figured out, there's a hiccup in the production line because the machinery malfunctions. There are just a slew of reasons that you can't get any further, and you terminate your relationship with this co-packer.

All that said . . .

You have to find a new small co-packer. You burned some inventory because some of the ingredients are now expired spoilage. You figured out how to fund this larger run, but the delays are too costly and the partnership breaks down.

Now you have no more choices. You have to find a new co-packer, but the only one you can find hasn't ever processed this kind of product, so you have to buy the equipment needed.

To **buy your own equipment**, turn to page 91

You found that you could lease a piece of equipment for a relatively inexpensive price, comparable to others you've seen. You sign the paperwork in hopes that it will be a good return on your investment.

This part can be really fun. You get to pick the exact equipment you want. You get to put all the specs in place so that it fits your needs. In a way, it's like the ultimate control (enjoy it while you can!), and in the end, you get a big, shiny new thing. Christopher Hesse, founder of Vukoo Nutrition, bought his own equipment thinking it would make his business easier. He didn't know it would come with a whole host of problems.

CASE STUDY

Christopher Hesse

I bought the equipment I needed but now I had to find a place to put it. Do you share a space in an existing co-packing plant? This wasn't ideal because they want us to go in for six hours in the middle of the night, on the off shift, after other clients were done with their shifts. We tried that, but another client at the co-packer was growing, so they didn't have room for us anymore.

> Now I have to find a new space. Sales must support the overhead, and here I am throwing $10,000 a month away to store my equipment. All the co-packers I looked at wanted to see 50,000–80,000 units being sold with a twelve-month history to support taking me on. There's no solution for new businesses who can't afford the overhead yet and cannot get to 50,000–100,000 units every four to six weeks.

But regardless of the risks, you pull the trigger and purchase your new equipment. There is always a pride of ownership when founders do this. Suddenly your whole business is now legit. You are official and you're feeling very competent. This is the machine that's going to get you to $40 million in revenue. You're on your way to build for scale now, baby.

But who has that kind of cash around at this stage in the game? You've had to take on some debt by now, and you are still sitting on all these perishable ingredients with orders that are looming over your head.

You pulled the trigger to order your beautiful new machine, but, unfortunately, as you might have guessed, there are delivery delays. It has to come from overseas on a ship. Maybe there was a boat stuck in the Suez Canal, a dockworkers' strike, a hurricane, or a simple miscommunication on deadlines. Whatever the reason, your installation is delayed. When it finally arrives, there are more delays to train the staff at the co-packer on how to run that piece of equipment. You travel there in person to train the workers yourself. It is your machine, after all. But then they experience some staff turnover after just a few weeks, and you have to go back again and retrain the new people.

All that said . . .

All of these delays lead up to no product, which leads up to no sales, and you are running out of cash. When you're out of cash, you have two decisions. You can raise money through loans to pay for the mounting overhead or you can pull out all the stops and do something drastic to try to stay in business.

Decision: Do you try something drastic or do you try to get a loan?

To **try something drastic**, turn to 94

To **try for a loan**, turn to 96

You Try Something Drastic

You still have a big order waiting to be filled and you're down to the wire. It's do or die time. You realize the only way that you're going to be able to fill that order is to compromise on the quality of your product. You're going to have to give up one of the ingredients that is hanging everything up.

So there is this—I hate to use the word—"compromise." You're going to have to come to grips with the fact that if you have the highest-level ingredients, you're going to have to charge a lot more to have a viable business, and you may not be getting the healthiest food to the broadest group of people. There is an *x* axis and a *y* axis, and at some point, if you lower your quality a bit—and I'm not saying it has to go to abysmal levels—you might be able to reach a broader audience.

What choice do you have? You adjust the recipe and it no longer meets your standards. Now you have a product that isn't the product that you wanted to sell. And you have a lot of it. You go to the retailer and explain what happened and tell them you are ready to place your product on their shelves. But they are disappointed that you are not delivering what you said you would. It turns out your recipe is pretty much the same thing that they already have, so they don't want it.

What do you do next? Do you give away that product before it expires and use it as a marketing gimmick to raise awareness for your brand, knowing it's subpar?

You need to move it before it expires or else it all gets pitched.

It has a three-week shelf life, so you find yourself selling the product out of the back of your car. You are giving it to everybody you know, you are in the hustle, taking whatever cash people are willing to pay.

Now you are scrambling with only a week left before it all goes bad. You try giving it to influencers. You're giving it to other grocery stores. Anything to get a sale. The thinking was that a dollar was better than nothing, but it didn't do anything for the business and it degraded the value of the brand. It was a last-ditch effort to recoup some costs that spiraled the drain. It was a Hail Mary pass.

This is not an uncommon story. On several occasions in my own CPG businesses, I have had to heavily discount product to liquidate it to get dollars in the door.

All that said . . .

Eventually you run out of product. Nothing worked. Every gimmick failed. You have no money for a second production run. You are still going to pay for the value of that machine. What choice do you have?

You give up.

After all the ups and downs, you throw in the towel. But you're still on the hook to pay for that equipment you'll never use. There's depreciation to the machine based on use. You have to pay for whatever that difference is. If it wasn't used at all, you can sell it for a little better price to the highest bidder.

You watch your piece of shiny equipment get hauled away, and you use what you get to pay off as much debt as you can. Then you retreat to lick your wounds and look for a job.

THE
END

You Try for a Loan

You've tapped out everything you have in savings. You've even dried up all your resources in terms of friends and family, so the only route you have left is to try to get a loan or find an investor.

No investor will touch you at this point. You are clearly a failing business that can show very few signs that a return is possible. You have no product, so you can't talk about product sales. You don't have any big corporate accounts to show that sales will come. This is a no-go.

As for loans, you look all over. There are many different sources of loans from private, commercial, and government institutions, but the problem is that you have no impressive record of sales. Most loans require a track record of at least two years.

You have a piece of equipment that is devaluing by the minute. There's no collateral elsewhere. You're hesitant to put any of your own personal collateral in because you don't see sales either. Honestly, you wouldn't lend to yourself.

All that said . . .

At the end of the day, you're considered not bankable.

This is where you have to pull out all the stops.

Make a list of every single resource you have.

You leverage your home, you pull your funds from your 401(k), your college savings, all of your stocks. You deplete every ounce of resources of time and money. These are costly and permanent constraints you now get to live with.

The trade-off is that you maintain your standards and your control and produce a quality product that generates interest from the consumers. It takes two or three times as long and four times as much money because you have to buy land or you have to find a place to rent.

When we say "facility," there's really a spectrum of what that can mean. Retrofitting a warehouse is an option if you don't want to build from the ground up. You can take over from somebody else who failed. You can rent a room in a bigger food company. I've used extra rooms in my friend's co-packing facilities to get my products up and going. I rented a twenty-by-twenty room for a little bit, and that saved me time because it was already in a facility with the right permits, insurance, and everything else. It even had the equipment. They had the warehousing and loading docks, pallets, all that stuff.

Once you find a location, you have to consider all the other logistical factors. The manufacturing facility has to be the right size. It has to have access for a truck to load. The electrical system has to be set up correctly for your equipment. You have to pay attention to zoning. Do you have to get a permit? Because you are creating a food-grade facility that will sell to corporate accounts, there are all kinds of government and health code regulations you need to learn and inspections you are required to have.

Now you have to think about buying the equipment and get to work mapping out the layout of the facility. It all has to flow and be efficient.

It's impossible to anticipate every hardship you will go through and everything that can go wrong. I recommend getting in touch with as many CPG factory owners as you can find. A really good resource right now is the Mid-Day Squares team. They have documented their entire journey—from doing business out of their condo to owning their own facility—and they have publicly shared it on social media and their podcast, *Mid-Day Squares Uncensored*.

CASE STUDY

Mid-Day Squares Founders

Nick Saltarelli, cofounder: "There was a line we said every day: 'When you find yourself on the side of the majority, stop and reflect.' What can we do that is radically different than the majority? One weird thing about the food industry, if you DON'T outsource your core competencies, you get laughed out of the room. Investors didn't want to fund our manufacturing when we went and told them we wanted

---

to build a manufacturing plant. But running the end-to-end process was our core competency! If we went to co-packers, we would end up with the same product as everyone else. Mid-Day Squares would not exist today if we didn't own our manufacturing plant. Full stop."

Lezlie Karls-Saltarelli, cofounder: "We almost fell to that temptation to scale and go to a co-packer. I toured twenty-six co-packers and not a single one worked. They'd give me the product that was supposed to be a square and it ended up being a circle. They said what I wanted was impossible. If it were up to the contract manufacturers, our product would look like every other product on the shelf. We had no choice but to figure this out ourselves, which led to an extreme investment in our plant and R&D line to keep our product as innovative as we wanted it to be. I used to say, 'If man can walk on the moon, we can figure out how to manufacture these squares.'"

All that said . . .

Thankfully for you, the outcome of this is that you are successful in generating interest, and people start getting behind your company. And you get some sales! You maintained the quality you knew you were going to achieve in the very beginning, and you benefit when people "vote" with their dollars and buy your product.

This leads you to the next decision. Are you going to keep growing fast or are you going to slow down? You know if you decide to grow fast, this is going to lead you to the venture capital route, which means giving up equity. If you slow down, you're not sure what that will look like, but you know it means you will do it on your own, the way you wanted all along.

Decision: Do you take it slow or do you raise funds from professional investors?

To **take it slow**, turn to page 101

To **raise funds from professional investors**, turn to page 134

The impact of this decision is that now that you own your facility, you don't have to worry so much about someone else's production schedules and targets. You get to make your own timeline, and you can rely on word-of-mouth networks for marketing. You must be patient, but you can eventually reach measurable success.

You can more or less make your product on the fly as orders come in. You can scale up and fulfill each order and then slow things down in between. You have a lot more control over the kind of destiny you want—to a certain degree. Of course, you still have overhead and orders and product to move, but there aren't the same constraints as when you sign with a co-packer.

Let's say you have a big day on the internet due to some special exposure and you sell a whole lot. You have the flexibility to meet that. Then, if that is followed closely by a retail account that wants more, you're not at the mercy of anyone but yourself.

You can even stage events now to hype up your brand and do things you never could do before you were independent. But if no orders come in, you're back to going door-to-door to local cafés and local retailers, trying to get your product picked up.

If you built your facility properly and you've used the right blend of debt and equity, you're not too terribly financially strained, as long as you have a certain level of sales. That means if you don't push it too hard, you're not going to overextend yourself. The key is patience. You let things build and are OK with just generating a little bit of income and working at improving your processes, working on the layout of your facility, and getting better pricing on ingredients. This is a time to tighten everything up and watch that bottom line.

All that said . . .

Big box does come knocking on your door and places a massive order. The biggest you've ever seen. Wonderful! Your goal was to make it big and this, for sure, is the big time. Are you ready for this? There's nothing wrong with continuing to grow slow and steady. Maybe another year or two would be better before you tackle such a monstrous task.

Decision: Do you say no or do you fulfill the big order?

To **say no**, turn to page 103

To **fulfill the order**, turn to page 105

Have a happy life! You pick excellence and predictability over risks.

You stay regional with a manageable business. The bonus is that you get really good at maintaining work/life balance. It's a great business. You don't get out over your skis. You're not overly indebted.

All that said . . .

The business will pay itself off at a certain point and provide enough profits later on that you are comfortable well into retirement. You're not a national brand like you hoped, but you're content with what you built.

Brands and founders say no to large accounts quite frequently because they know the operational lift and they can't fulfill it. You don't have to take on accounts. Or you can walk before you run. Retailers do understand this.

When we launched the honeycomb business, we had a national retailer that wanted to launch us in over a thousand stores. There was no way we could have done that operationally. I might have been able to line up the cash. I might have been able to produce the goods, but it would have hurt the rest of the business. We just didn't have the means to do that, so we started with twenty stores. Then we moved to thirty. It's OK to say, "We can't do that." Everyone gets so excited that this is going to be their big launch. I have not experienced this first-hand. I avoided the trap because I know enough founders who took the bait, and I am avoiding the misery.

THE END

Caveat: This opportunity was not a once-in-a-lifetime kind of deal. As Nathaniel, your original purpose keeps coming back, and you get itchy. You know you won't be satisfied until you go national. The next time a big-box offer comes along, you can say yes.

You decide that whatever it takes, you're doing this thing.

As enticing as big contracts sound, they sink the battleship more often than not. There are a couple of retailers I won't name by name, but they're notorious for taking on a smaller brand that doesn't sell through, and then they send the product back and it bankrupts the company.

People forget that while you can have an order for ten thousand units or ten thousand cases or whatever it is, you have to actually produce all those goods. Often it takes sixty to ninety days to get paid on that order.

You have to order more ingredients and hire and pay for more staff to increase production, not to mention the increased time, electricity, water, and all the other stuff you need to produce those goods. When you are done, you put it on a truck and it goes to that retailer and you wait to get paid. Do you have enough extra cash to cover all of this?

But that isn't all. You have to provide signage, samples, demos, discounts, promotions, contests, and digital support to roll out a new product in their store. It's not just getting it in the door when it comes to the big box. Oh no.

They expect all the promotions for this snazzy new food to come from the brand. You better hope you have enough margin to do that because if you've given them a price that doesn't allow you the cash to promote, you are sunk. You must have a marketing budget. You can't simply send the product without signage or displays. Very rarely will a retailer let you launch a new product without some sort of promotion. They don't want the risk. And neither do you. You want the thing to perform.

Suddenly you're in the negative because of all these unforeseen costs. Plus, you're marketing to them at a price that doesn't allow much margin.

Again, the keys here are margin and consumption. Everyone wants a product that has a profitable margin to be consumed at a high volume. So you look around and see that nobody else is doing product sampling. You want your product to move off the shelf, but it's a new thing. Customers haven't seen it before. They might have questions about it. You need to do whatever it takes just to get your product moving.

The usual commentary in this situation is that it's one thing to get into a store. It's another to get into the basket. It's another thing to get checked out. And it's a whole other thing to get repurchased a second time.

Consider these the gates of successes. You got into the store, great, but did somebody pick it up? Did they actually go through the check-out? How often do we see items that people picked up and then put back on the shelf or on a different shelf somewhere else?

The crucial indicator of success is if they repurchase. That's when you've got that second order coming in from the store and then that third order coming in. That's really when you understand if this market is going to work for you.

But as all of this happens, cash gets super strained. It's a tremendous marketing budget. It's a cash vacuum because you have to be able to sustain that for forty-five to sixty days. Sometimes up to ninety.

Many times there's a distributor involved, and they are notorious for not paying on time. If a distributor is in the loop, that's another 20 percent margin you have to give up. You better hope that you've priced your product right to allow for a retailer markup, a distributor markup, perhaps a broker fee, marketing budget, and the actual cost of production before you get your first payment.

Cash flow is king, they say. It can be an absolute bear, and a taxing of your soul. I personally admire businesses that function autonomously and generate their own funding, that are able to create enough profit to sustain themselves to live another day.

This is the point where a lot of times companies will just give up because they can't sustain this kind of loss. Or they go back and pull out of the deal. They realize they can't make a profit. Sometimes they won't break even.

All that said . . .

You fall into the same trap that so many other new companies fall into. You do everything you can to make it work, but retailers are notorious for not taking on the risk if a product doesn't sell.

They give your product a month to move off the shelves, but if it doesn't sell the way they want it to, they send it back to you and demand a credit or withhold funds for future payments.

Now you're stuck with aging or expired inventory that you can't sell elsewhere. The retailer has not paid you yet, so they shortchange the invoice. You don't get paid at all, or maybe you get paid a fraction of what you thought you were going to get.

You've wasted a bunch of inventory, and you don't have a proof point to go to the next retailer and say, "Look, this worked out well." You can't. It's really hard to get out of that hole.

Good luck. That's tough.

Christopher Hesse, founder of Vukoo Nutrition, said, "I started this business ten years ago, when I was twenty-two, and now I'm thirty-two. It took four years of patience to get set up the way I need to be. It feels like managing two businesses (the brand and the manufacturing), so it can be hard to keep a healthy balance alone. You need someone to oversee accounts and other stuff."

→ Turn the page

I hate to tell you this now and risk dashing your hopes, but here is the ending for 98–99 percent of all brand-new CPG companies: whammy.

The buyer didn't show up, trends moved. Every excuse in the book is used as to why somebody didn't want to buy your company. Metrics that mattered yesterday don't matter today. Usually it won't happen overnight. It'll be a super slow, long-drawn-out thing. It'll test your mettle. You'll tell yourself you've been forged. You did your best. You gambled. But this time you lost.

It just feels like an absolute waste of time. All your staff has to be let go. People are incredibly sad (or mad). They believed in you; they believed in the product. And now they are watching as the company they passionately helped you build is sold off in parts to the highest bidder.

Or perhaps it will live on as portions of itself in the marketplace. But you won't be involved. You'll see little hints of it maybe in a brand that it evolved into, or a product category that you had thought about. The grocery store will be miserable for you for a while.

THE END

Veronica's
PATH

You Are Now Veronica

The category you have landed on with Perfect Power Pickles is something that would be considered a wide-open white space. There isn't anything truly of this nature. It is one of those category creators, something like a Poo-Pourri or Wonderful Pistachios. Where there's no defined path ahead, category creators have their own set of problems. They can be incredibly successful. Or they never get off the ground.

For those in the marketplace who just haven't seen anything like this, they don't know how to deal with it. They don't know where to place it on a shelf; they don't know what to charge for it. It takes a lot of trust in your vision, while also listening to others and adapting because you can't push on all fronts and break the mold everywhere. It's a "know when to hold them, know when to fold them, know when to play within the rules" kind of deal.

You research the pickle market, learning about pickle production and sourcing and importing. You know, all things pickle. The more you learn, the more you realize that this is a large category that has not been disrupted in a very long time. There is a very small group of three or four incumbents, which are household names, pantry staples. Nothing has come onto the market to challenge them since they were founded generations ago.

Do you feel confident enough in your product and the demand to tackle these major players? Are you up for the challenge? If you are, you could have the potential for creating a whole new category of pickle. It can be placed in the pickle aisle, sure, but it can also go with energy supplementation products, with exercise snacks, and even in the diabetic foods section.

You know this is going to take a significant amount of capital, and as luck would have it, you have shared your plan with just the right people at the right time.

Your friends and family want to invest in Perfect Power Pickles.

Decision: Do you turn down the money or take it?

To **turn down the money**, turn to page 113

To **take the money**, turn to page 114

You didn't take the money and choose not to grow your company. You decide to keep things small.

There are many reasons why a founder would choose to say no to investors. As an MBA graduate, you are aware of the long, stressful road that lies ahead, particularly if you are a category creator. No one else has forged the path for you to follow, and you may decide you would rather avoid the headache.

The loyal fan base for your product is sufficient to sustain local growth, and you may be able to stock in a few regional grocery stores one day, but you have to figure out how to ramp up your production if you are going to do that. Right now, your small apartment kitchen is maxed out. You know the hassle it will be.

All that said . . .

You've decided that Perfect Power Pickles will not become the challenger to the pickle industry or the category creator that it has the potential to be. Rather, you will continue to produce and sell locally.

Go to Angela's path and start a local food business on page 27

You Take the Money

You have made the decision to go with this as a business opportunity, so you're going to take this money from family and friends. This round of raising money is not considered venture capital (VC) yet, but we'll get there.

Disclaimer! Nothing you read here should be taken as legal advice. I am not a lawyer, and I am speaking from personal opinion and personal experience.

When you take money from others, you often take it in exchange for equity in your company. This means dilution. When you dilute by taking money from others, you are selling a portion of the company, which means you no longer own 100 percent.

These are friends and family who believe in you and in the product. Losing equity to them is not a huge concern when it comes to control and decision-making. They're not professional and they don't expect to take over your role. They're on board with your vision, so they are willing to put in little checks here and there.

It's not life-changing money, and as a result there isn't a ton of risk for them. Sometimes it's a thousand dollars. Sometimes it's ten thousand. Maybe even a hundred thousand. But at the end of the day, you've made that decision to take their money, and you're not going to own 100 percent of your company anymore.

You start with 100 percent ownership available. The more ownership you give up, the more money you raise, the smaller and smaller your piece of the pie gets. When it's a friends-and-family round of fundraising, you may only give up 10 percent of the company. Sometimes more, sometimes less.

If you're going to accept money from grandma or your roommate, there are ways to go about accepting those funds. There are legal documents that will probably need to be drawn up. You can sell direct equity; you can sell something called a convertible note, which is kind of like a loan, but then it converts to equity over a period of time. You could spend the time to hire attorneys and lawyers and document it all up formally and spend a lot of money on that.

Or you could do it a little cheaper and document the loan yourself using templates from the internet. Sometimes this round will just include straight loans without worrying about equity. If it's your grandma, for example, it will probably just be a loan, clean and simple. Personally, any time I could take a loan from a friend, I'd go with that. Then I'm not giving up any ownership. If it's a friendly loan, you pay them back sometime. Maybe there's a time frame, usually two or three years at a decent percentage rate between 10 and 12 percent. That sort of thing.

I mean, if someone's going to loan me money and not tell me when to pay them back, I'm going to take the money, and I'm not going to bring it up again until I have the money to repay them. That's the honest truth. But I have never come across an occasion when that's happened. There's usually some sort of question at the get-go like, "When do you think you can pay me back?"

But the point here is that you've taken a fork in the road. From now on, expect that people will ask more questions than before. You will have to explain some of your actions now that you didn't before. Not that you have to defend them, necessarily, but people will be curious if you have made money yet and will want to know how things are going.

When you start becoming more of a professional company, those things can bite you in the behind. Especially if you lack documentation early on. I suggest that shortly after some measure of success, you professionalize your relationships. You clearly delineate the terms of every loan: when and if it's going to convert to equity, repayment schedule, and anything else that is relevant. I would guess 99 percent of the time people don't do that to start, which is fine to a certain point, but the minute there's either a hiccup or a success, things change.

You need to have some type of accounting system. For instance, you can learn some sort of accounting software program or you can use an outside accounting firm. This decision doubles back to your intention for the company. Is this a business like Angela's, where you want to just go to a farmers' market and someone wants to give you a loan to buy a tent? You probably don't need legal papers for that sort of thing. Pay them back as soon as you can and you're all good. But when you get into higher dollar amounts for bigger companies, you may want to start having some expert help on the financial side of things.

Let's say you are just looking to spend some money on marketing. That's a little riskier because you can spend all your money on marketing and never see return of that cash. It's very different than buying a physical asset like a table for a farmers' market or a machine for a co-packer facility.

You know this is going to be a much broader business opportunity than it is now because you are going to take on the classic pickle big brands. So you have to raise money and you need to do it right. You are going professional, which means you think through the appropriate documentation from the start. You get lawyers to help you properly draw up convertible notes and other loans from everyone who approaches you with money.

My family never does business together, so I don't know if this is a good or bad policy. In my family, they always have the right to speak their mind, but I always have the right to ignore their suggestions. But I have heard of others who operate differently.

Seeing you as a true professional makes your family really proud, and your aunt approaches you with a gift of $1,000. This does happen in real life and when it does, I suggest you take it and say thank you, regardless of the amount. Show your gratitude by giving them free product. Include them in newsletters and events. Involve them in the process. Don't just take the money and run. But if it's a gift, it does not give them the right to speak their mind in terms of how you run your business.

No matter how you look at it, starting a business will have an effect on all of your personal relationships. Vanessa Dew, cofounder of Health-Ade, shared how the pressures of being a start-up affected her life and relationships with her family.

CASE STUDY

Vanessa Dew

The first place we went to for funding/loans were our friends and family. They became our first investors. They were fans of the brand but, most of all, they were rooting for us. Back then, I was going to school and holding down a nine-to-five job. I worked at a Fortune 50 company, which was cushy and dependable, but not at all fulfilling. My best friend, her husband,

and I started an entrepreneur club because business was our thing. We were going to bail on our corporate jobs and give back to the world and find a way to be more personally fulfilled. But we had to pay the bills. I worked the corporate job for two years while going to school and building our new business, Health-Ade. I took out a personal student loan to fund my life with a runway for one year to quit my job and go all in with Health-Ade, which was making no money at the time but had some real energy and momentum behind it.

When I told my parents that I was going to quit my well-paying job to run this business, they thought I was depressed and maybe needed to be put in an institution because I was talking crazy. My mother even put together a spreadsheet detailing my projected salary loss and other opportunity costs I would lose by doing this. She sat down and said, "Look at what you're giving up here!"

I remember so vividly one night I was on my way to a birth-day party, and I stopped at a gas station in Hollywood. I was crying hysterically to my parents on the phone, pleading with them to see my point of view, and asking them to ultimately give their support. At the end of it I said, "Look, I'm going to do it, no matter what. You're either with me or not." I knew their point of view and that they didn't really agree, but it didn't stop me.

Eventually they warmed up to it. My dad even came and sold our kombucha with me once at a farmers' market, and my mom sewed the tablecloths for our tables.

Fast-forward to eight years later, my parents ended up investing in our company and are some of our biggest fans. But the real telltale sign of support was when my dad called my office phone. I didn't think he even knew that number. He told me he was proud of me and that he loved me. I was like, "I love you too, but who are you and what did you do with my father?!" That was really nice that it all came full circle.

All that said . . .

So now you have the funds, and because you have a day job and you are busy, you have the ability to bring on help. Do you hire one person to help you, because you are now big enough that you can't do it all on your own, or do you find an agency to guide you?

Decision: Do you bring on one person to help, or an agency?

To **hire an agency**, turn to page 120

To **hire one person**, turn to page 125

You Hire an Agency

You have raised a bunch of money, so you can go in and hire a really expensive agency that does fabulous work.

If you're looking to find an agency, somebody always has a friend who does marketing. It usually starts by asking a couple of friends and leads to somebody somewhere saying, "I worked at this agency," or "I know a guy . . ."

If you absolutely have no contacts in the marketing world, a good place to start is to do a quick search using keywords like "consumer packaged goods branding agencies." Check what awards they have won for branding, design, marketing, and food. There are also agency associations you can look to.

Ultimately you will put out what's called a "Request for Proposal" (RFP). If you're going this route, your RFP will collect a dozen or a half dozen agency submissions. You'll review them and check the references. Look at their past case studies and everything that helps you get a sense for whether they are a good fit. They'll all present their best face, but in my experience, they are all almost interchangeable. You'll call the references and, no surprise, they will have nothing but great things to say. So you'll end up going with your gut on one of them.

Agencies can bring a lot of value to the table for a much lower cost than hiring a dozen people as employees of your company. You get broad expertise, which brings with it a broader understanding of the marketing climate and your specific category. They have far more resources, they have far more staff, they have far more knowledge, they're able to tap into the inner workings of the industry, and they keep their knowledge relevant. They also bring key partnerships to the table that maybe wouldn't be accessible if you had not gone with them. An agency is a fast track to getting resources and knowledge.

But you know that it all comes at a cost. I've taken that bait several times. I should admit that, personally, I am not a fan of agencies for a start-up. And definitely not for something that's unique, because I don't think you get that nimbleness you need. Their thinking tends to be almost prescriptive: "This is how it's done." No room for creativity or innovation.

Of course there are the creative groups, but they cost ungodly sums of money, which, again, just doesn't make sense for a start-up.

But don't let my opinions sway you. If you're looking to build a team and ramp up with a great website that tracks marketing reach and contacts, one that includes tight blog posts with search engine optimization and that kind of stuff, an agency will help you do that. The alternative is to try to learn all that yourself or to hire out each task individually. It will take much longer. Ultimately, if you're looking to speed to market, an agency is a great resource.

All agencies do—particularly marketing agencies—is take two numbers (the numerator and a denominator) and create another number. Obviously, there's work behind it, and they are providing you with some reports that are really just a numerator and a denominator. So many entrepreneurs don't poke holes into what the numerator is or what the denominator is. They just take the final answer as gospel. This is good in the short term as it's a way to outsource some of the thinking, but it's certainly nothing a founder couldn't already do himself or herself. That said, I do like the temporary nature of agencies. If you have to cancel your contract with them, you're not destroying someone's livelihood as you would be if you had to let go of an employee.

—Matt Matros, founder of Protein Bar,

Limitless, and Shopflix Studios

So you pick an agency. It's a whizzbang, great experience for a while. The team is very responsive. They help you get up on your feet and you're excited. But then the pushback starts when you have innovative ideas. They begin to be less responsive to you. You begin to feel like they're discouraging your creativity. The bills pile up. The tensions are a little high, and you notice lower performance.

When there isn't an initial success, the agency becomes very encumbered with their thinking, and they don't have the passion you have. You're just another account, so they don't allocate the resources for you to really work through problems. I have not found an agency that has rolled up their sleeves and gotten in the muck and thought truly creatively and strategically in a cost-effective manner. It seems like they just always want to lower your price and double your marketing budget, which is garbage in my opinion.

I have heard it from every agency I've known. "Oh, your price is too high. You haven't marketed enough." I haven't yet found an agency that thinks about return on investment of their actions. And when you ask them for accountability, it's always a nebulous conversation because they can't truly measure all marketing dollars and what did or did not drive sales. It's brutal.

So you can spend more, as they advise, but you're not seeing income. People are starting to use the word "scale" around you ad nauseum. You're sold this grand vision and it just burns cash. It's like you're being sold a Ferrari when you just need a skateboard. It doesn't make sense. Sometimes good enough is good enough.

All that said . . .

You can no longer justify the expense of the agency, so you part ways.

You still have a lot of work to do and a new decision needs to be made about what expenses you can and cannot justify. You know you can't do it yourself, so you either need to hire one person who can share the load or try to raise enough money to bring on a team of people. Your costs are a major consideration because you've just burned a bunch of cash with the agency, and you don't have anything to show for it in terms of your revenues.

Time to bring in the cavalry. You need to hire some help, but where to find it? I'm consistently shocked at what comes out from shaking the little network tree. Many times somebody either knows someone directly or knows somebody who knows somebody. Those conversations lead to a lot of insight and great contacts.

People are offering unsolicited assistance to help support you—maybe it's a videographer, key influencers, lawyers, who knows? People are starting to come out of the woodwork, and they want to support you. You've gotten the business to that level. And that's incredibly gratifying.

Now that you have a little bit of learning under your belt and you want to hire those contract employees, and you have a clearer vision of your destination, you have to determine which areas of the business are in most need of some supplemental help.

You have enough money to afford one person, but also you sure could use a whole team of qualified people right about now. To do that, you would have to raise money from professional investors.

Decision: Do you hire one person or raise funds from professional investors?

To **hire one person**, turn to page 125

To **raise funds from professional investors**, turn to page 134

You want to stay conservative and just bring on one person to start with, and maybe later add a whole team.

But what kind of person should you hire? Understanding yourself is key. Try to discover what you're best suited to do and what you might want to learn, and hire someone with skills that complement your own. One founder I know offered wise advice on this topic.

> *Don't hire someone to do something that you can do yourself. Learn what that job is first, and then when you do hire it out, you'll know more about what the job is and what makes it work or not work. Hire after two things have happened: (1) There's been some level of pain. The pain is usually because the organization as a whole is being slowed down or you, personally, just get too busy and can't do it all anymore. (2) You've tried to do it and you know what it takes. Try to hire after you have done it yourself for a while.*
>
> **—Matt Matros, founder of Protein Bar,**
> **Limitless, and Shopflix Studios**

You can either hire someone who is an expert or someone who is less experienced. Do you almost double down and put more cash into somebody, a single individual, who is more of a utility player, bringing with them a great deal of industry experience? Or are you just looking for somebody who can help work shoulder-to-shoulder with you and grind through things—someone who can be a second set of hands and eyes and a sounding board, who may not have the experience yet but will save you money?

Back when my cofounders and I were running Health-Ade as a start-up, we did everything ourselves and we were embedded in every decision. That was fine for a while, but we soon found that we couldn't do everything and in fact, there were gaps we needed to hire for. It was hard to shift from focusing on the day-to-day and letting some of that go. It took some self-reflection and discovery along the journey for all of us, but at the end of the day we are actually able to do more with an empowered team.

—Vanessa Dew, cofounder of Health-Ade

All that said . . .

You have another decision to make. Do you want an expert who can bring wise counsel and a been-there-done-that perspective or someone who is young and eager and isn't already entrenched in the industry?

Decision: Do you hire an expert or a junior?

To **hire an expert**, turn to page 127

To **hire a junior**, turn to page 130

You go with someone who is senior, who brings a level of expertise that is specific to some level of your company, and who worked for a big global conglomerate.

Experts are great. You really like this person. They know everything about CPG. They're at the point in their career where they know so much that they are truly an authority. Usually, you hire them as a consultant and set up a monthly retainer with them, and so there goes $4,500 to $5,500 a month. They tell you they will lower their rates for you because you are a start-up, but they want equity in the company in exchange so they can really be part of the success, to align interests.

You think this is great. This person knows it all. They know everybody. They're going to open up doors to bring in money and raise funds. They are going to fix all your problems. Of course they should have some equity in your company! Note that this can be anywhere from 1 to 10 percent or more. But you think it will be totally worth it because they will give you their expert advice. They've shown you a list of wins they have had in their career, and you are confident they will take you to the next level.

In my experience, this is very rarely worth it. You'll spend more time drawing up the contract than actually working with the person, and you'll just end up having to kick them out.

They will show you all the successes they've had, but they will rarely show you their losses. Any good financial disclosure always states that past performance is no indication of future success.

I'm not going to say that there is no place for experts. There certainly is. But if you hire an expert too early, you will very likely run into problems. They cost a lot of money and often just give advice you can't implement yet. I've noticed experts don't seem to want to get down in the weeds and really do the work. Unfortunately, if it's a part-time gig and they are really at an advanced stage in their career, there's a resistance to actual work. You don't find them picking up a phone, writing memos, sending emails, or generally getting things done. Of course, this isn't always the case. Just most often.

Instead, they focus a lot on strategy. But strategy without implementation or execution is worthless. Ideas are a dime a dozen, as they say. They just want to think and tell you what to do. And I can't blame them. They have worked their butts off in their career, and they've gotten to a point where they can direct teams of people now. They are usually incredibly brilliant.

But to step off the brilliance pedestal and get into the dirt, to get things done, is not the skill they bring. And when they do, the execution always seems to be lacking, or it's dated. You can't take a high-performing executive who is used to managing a team of three hundred and plug them into a team of two. You don't have the same resources. You can't execute their brilliant ideas because you don't have the people to enact the vision. So now there is tension that you never support their big vision. There's a mismatch, a misalignment of strategy and tactical execution based on available resources. What you've really done is hire somebody who gives you more opinions.

You know by now that everyone feels they have to have an opinion. You're three months in and you realize you're not really getting anything done. When you ask why, your new expert will tell you it takes a while to understand what's going on with the business. They say that there is always a three-month ramp. That's why you've contracted them for six months. So you are patient for six months, and you have all these great strategies and ideas, but still you see no way to get those ideas done. And now you're even more out of money.

Talk to yourself. Good enough is good enough, no? Your goal here is to live another day. It's not to sell for a $100 million tomorrow.

You are having second thoughts. Maybe it is time to edit. It's time to let the expert go and possibly relearn some things yourself. But before you cut that string, you have to think about what agreements you made when you brought them on. Can you get out of the contract so easily? Did you give them 5 percent equity in your company? Yikes.

All that said . . .

You figure out how to part ways amicably. It's always a good idea to stay on civil terms with people. They do have a lot of connections in the industry, after all.

The hard thing is that you have given up equity to somebody who didn't perform and who raided the coffers. It was just a miss. A mismatch of strategy and execution.

You say good riddance to that expensive, knowledgeable help who wasn't helpful. You don't feel too bad because you have been able to cut down the learning curve. Sure, maybe that expert didn't work out, but in the meantime you've gained some valuable experience. You've expedited your ability to understand the function of your business.

Now you don't have a choice because paying the expert depleted your funds. You have to raise money to stay in business. And you still need help.

To **hire a junior**, turn to page 130

You Hire a Junior

To keep within your budget, you may have to get somebody who's a little younger. You find someone who doesn't have as much experience, but what they lack in history they make up for in enthusiasm and commitment. The word that people use is "hungry."

You want to find someone who can learn alongside you. Someone who you can educate. You find a person who can grow with the company and is a good cultural fit. They bring the added advantage of some ancillary experience from another industry, a core skill set that's applicable and can be replicated in the food and beverage business.

> Get somebody who maybe just graduated in project management or has done some of that. Schedule meetings two or three times a week to keep you on track. If you can't get something done, that person can also help out and do some of the tasks. I've started many businesses, and as an entrepreneur what typically happens is that you try to do everything but then it takes so much longer to hit your target. My daughter was learning project management so I hired her right from the start with my cookie business. Because of her organization and assistance, we were able to get into the local farmers' market within two months. That would've never happened otherwise.
>
> **—Nina Jolic, cofounder of enci sweets**

It's a great feeling when you hand off things you're not best suited to do or are plain miserable at. I personally hate dealing with social media, but I know that it's a great way to market, so that is one of the first things that I typically hand off.

But with that said, I have learned not to hand things off too soon. If I could make one very strong suggestion in this regard, don't let pain avoidance drive your decisions. In my desire to remove myself from things that pain me, I have let go of the reins too early and haven't really learned the lessons I needed. I haven't really understood the marketplace enough before I handed things over. Then I'm beholden to the people I've turned things over to because now they are the experts on my company. It doesn't feel good.

You have to understand what you want. There isn't a standard playbook for who to hire and when. Even if you're going into a category that's highly competitive with a lot of different brands, your brand story is unique. Your why, your who, they're all unique to you.

You also need enough self-awareness to know what key roles you are not good at and what you're not enjoying. Do you need somebody who is willing to manage systems and processes and be sort of like the traffic coordinator for your business? Or maybe (like me) you need someone to manage social media or finance or customer service.

As a founder who started a company out of thin air, I can say there are things that drain and things that invigorate. To be managing customer complaints and irrational comments on the internet is incredibly taxing for me. Some people take it as a challenge or even enjoy bringing resolution to those sorts of things. But for me that is a miserable experience. I like processes and systems, but I don't particularly like to manage projects because I am not super in the weeds when it comes to details. So those are positions I usually fill early on.

You want to bring on someone who can be a right-hand person, an extension, and the complement of yourself. But with that said, do be very careful. People tend to walk into a pitfall when they hire somebody who's just like them. It's exciting in the beginning because you're both talking about what excites you, but then at the end of the day, you both want to be CEO. You're too similar.

Make sure to take time clearly defining roles and responsibilities and expectations before you start to divide and conquer. When you have a small team, you just get things done. But if there are no real clear lanes, it gets muddied when there are mistakes and failure because no one knows who's responsible. This also happens when there is success. Everyone's laying claim to that success.

The work is beginning to encroach on your health and well-being. To maintain wellness, you have to bring someone on because you still have a life to live and you can't work twenty-four hours a day.

All that said . . .

So you bring someone on board and your decision works out. You think it through carefully and find someone who brings the skills you need and complements you in all the right ways. They stick with you and carry legacy knowledge from the early stages of the company. This is your first employee who stays with you through the long haul. You are smart enough to set up all the legal stuff on the first day so your relationship works out for the duration.

As you two become more effective and efficient, the company grows. Success is in view, but what is the next step? You guessed it. If you want to move fast, you have to raise more money.

For your second round of fundraising, you have tapped out all your friends and family, so now it's time to approach professional investors. By "professionals," I mean people who are looking for a return and aren't giving it to you because they love you.

To **raise funds from professional investors**, turn to page 134

You Raise Funds from Professional Investors

For this second round of raising money, you are now connecting with professional investors looking to maximize returns, which means you will be expected to make the most amount of money in the shortest amount of time. It's difficult to raise funds at this round. According to venture industry data, of all companies that take money from friends and family, only 48 percent manage to raise a second round. But keep in mind that when you take this money, you could be giving up 30 percent of your company on top of what you already gave away in the first round. You are dangerously close to losing control of your company.

Previously as the company was growing, your friends and family who believe in the product were just looking for a moderate return on their investment. They wanted something better than putting their money in a savings account, and it was exciting for them. They like the idea of saying that they are an investor in a food company. There's a playfulness to it.

Now when the company achieves a certain amount of scale, you start to be courted by professional investors. These investors can be a huge asset. They can bring operational expertise. They usually have great relationships in your industry. They can get you into hundreds, even thousands of retailers.

But you want to go big. You know the other side of that is to go home, right? And that tends to be where this shakes out. You've made the decision. You want to be a household brand. You want to get as big as possible, as fast as possible, and sell for the largest amount of money. Hundreds and hundreds of millions of dollars, which is doable.

It's funding that is the tricky part. The bigger you get, the more product you have to produce, the more cost of sales comes in. A CPG company is a voracious consumer of cash, especially if you are growing fast. The good thing is that there are groups out there looking for these kinds of investment opportunities.

Many times, you'll hear the term "VC" to refer to venture capitalists. These are professional investors who tend to get a lot of the fanfare. They know that one in a hundred of their investments will hit. And when I say "hit," I mean return a ton of cash. They're OK with losing on the individual deals, knowing that a few of the big investments will return all the cash to the fund.

Professional investors are looking for big market opportunities with very fast growth. A lot of times, they don't want the extra profits. They want to see profits plowed back into growth, so when you take money from them, you will be compromising your profitability for growth. Venture capital investors will expect you to grow 30 percent month over month rather than 30 percent a year, and that can be a daunting prospect and is nearly impossible to do. There are very few companies that get that right, and when they do, they consume a TON of money.

A lot of the time, you'll be running negative economics. You'll be growing faster than your cash supply, which means you're going to have to raise more and more funds. You're going to see this play out again and again on this path.

Ultimately, when you're out raising money, an investment boils down to risk, return, and timeline. What is that person or organization's appetite for risk? Are they tolerant of high risks or are they risk averse? What are their expectations on returns? Are they looking for a moderate return or something that's off the charts? In what time-line are they expecting this?

Venture capital tends to look for variables. Actually, strike that. Not "tends to." Their mandate is to find really high returns in a short period of time, which means they're more risky than someone who's looking for very moderate returns over a longer period of time.

A lot of the traditional business metrics can get skewed in this process. The best way to put this is that the cost of capital will never be returned the entire time you have that customer, which sounds weird. The cost you pay to acquire a new customer is more than that new customer will ever spend on your products. You'll be running negatively. But consider that when you have large scale, you can actually make those kinds of situations work. The question is: Can you get to scale?

As you start to grow and need to consume even more cash, your initial venture capital partner may not have the funds available to reinvest, which sometimes can be a bad signal to the marketplace. The fact is you're looking for rocket fuel for your rocket. But the rocket can fizzle.

No matter what you do, though, if you've been selling regionally, it's pretty likely you'll be contacted by teams of people, investors from large retailers and organizations looking for opportunities. They'll find you on social media. They'll find your product in the store. They'll find you at pitch contests, which are usually regional in nature, where you can go and present in front of a group of investors who have been curated and brought to a venue.

They have pitch contests at colleges and in most large communi-ties. It doesn't specifically have to be a food pitch contest. With that said, I don't normally advise taking too much time with these. It can be a tremendous time sink. You spend two, three months preparing for the event, talking to people, getting a presentation together, and all the while you're not focused on your business.

On that note, fundraising is a distraction in general. So many times it doesn't even bear any fruit. You join all the industry organizations and attend their networking events, but rarely does much come of it. Once you're at a certain level of success, trust that they will find you.

Once a professional investor contacts you, take a minute to learn about them. Look at their website and take note of the household brands they've invested in. Chances are, they have had huge successes that are really impressive. This makes it really hard to turn them down.

Then they offer big checks. Three, four, five, ten, fifteen, twenty, thirty million dollars can be yours to allow you to build this dream as big as possible. You can reach for anything under the sun you've ever thought about. They will provide that for you. They will give you a pathway to achieve your dreams. Who would say no to that?!

But what people don't realize is that when you take outside money, you are not truly in alignment with investors. They weren't there when you were starting your company. They don't really care about the quality and ingredients and health and wellness the way you do. The sole purpose of professional investors is to generate returns.

So you have conflicting motivators. Accepting money from friends and family was one thing. It helped you get over a hump or move to the next level. Accepting investment money means you are essentially stepping onto a hamster wheel, and that puts you on a rocket ship. It is a fast ride that has a 1 to 2 percent chance of success.

It's a pressure cooker that lasts five to eight years. All you can think about is grow, grow, grow, grow, grow, and hope you sell to somebody bigger than you, or list an IPO (initial public offering). We won't get to that point quite yet, but trust me, it's coming. Chris Hunter, founder of Four Loko and Koia, offered some advice based on his experience with professional investment.

CASE STUDY

Chris Hunter

Don't be solely focused on sales. Revenue is the rising tide that lifts all boats, but there are rocks and snags under the water no matter how high the tide gets.

Growth covers up so many sins. In my first company, we were not willing to give up the key responsibilities and that is exhausting. I guess you could say that's a young person's game. In my second company, I raised money to hire a highly qualified team early. But that's not always the best answer either. The more money you raise, the greater the chance of failure.

Every time I raised money, my decision was based mostly on who would give me the highest valuation. That wasn't always the wisest choice.

In my first company, for our first round of raising money, we raised funds from friends and family, SBA loans, credit cards.

Bootstrapping forced us to make some hard decisions like firing people we liked. We were forced to innovate as a last effort. Looking back, I'm so glad we didn't have money then because we'd have blown it all. It's too easy to be careless. It's better to learn lessons on $100 than on $100,000.

Later, we were approached by a VC. We were on a crazy growth run and they wanted to give us $15 million to "take some chips off the table" and put into our accounts. We said no. Shortly after, we got sued by multiple government agencies and went deep into debt. We regretted not taking the money. In the end, it all worked out for the best, but those need to be well-thought-out decisions to consider all the "what-ifs."

In most industries, big companies will have an effect on regulations, which will also affect smaller companies. We didn't get involved in the industry. We really should have taken the time to get to know the regulators, the associations, and other things like that. Get linked with partners who are in the industry you are in.

We survived and were good, but that was a pivotal moment. Don't dismiss money so fast because anything can (and will) happen.

All that said . . .

You are offered funds from an investor you feel good about, and you decide that this is the way you want to grow. Accountability is key. Once you've made that decision to raise funds, your world changes—not only the exercise of going through the fundraising, but the types of individuals you welcome into your organization, what level of control they may or may not have. These are all points for negotiation.

The next decision that comes is how do you use the funds? Your investors will have opinions about this, but since you are the one creating your adventure here, you get to pick. Three choices are before you now that you have enough money to do anything you want:

1. Bring on a full team to build out the infrastructure of the business.
2. Invest in a facility.
3. Invest in marketing.

Decision: Do you invest in a team, operations (facility), or marketing?

To **build your team**, turn to page 141

To **build a facility**, turn to page 145

To **invest in marketing**, turn to page 147

So you've gotten this large chunk of change, and you feel that you're best positioned to be the visionary and the driver of the agenda of the business with a full team.

After some consideration, you decide your team should include a marketing director, a salesperson, a finance director, and an operations manager. These are the key roles, but there are others you know you will want to bring on board at some point, including a designer, more people in marketing, a writer, and a PR/social media manager. You hope to be able to move the salesperson up eventually to head of sales and bring in a team under them. Then you'll try to find a broker.

You can see how the overhead can get quite big quite quickly. Salary adds up fast, especially if you get anybody who has any merit. Unless sales start coming in to justify all those bodies, you are playing a dangerous game, promising everyone that growth is on the horizon.

Too often founders make these kinds of decisions on the fly. Their justification is that if they put the team in place, that will generate the income to support the growth. If you just put the right people in the right positions, they're the ones who are going to get you there. But you have to ask yourself if it is wise to build so quickly before sales match expenses. There's a tension of growth vs. profits. Sometimes it works. Sometimes it doesn't.

> *I always had the vision that I wanted this company to be big so that we could change the landscape of childhood nutrition and bring our product to as many children as possible. In order to achieve this vision, I knew that I was going to have to bring on different people who had experience and connections in the industry. People with different skill sets. We did give*

more equity in the very beginning than I would have liked, but I don't ever regret giving the right equity to the right partners because it was able to accelerate the company to the vision I held of it. We wouldn't have gotten here as quickly if we hadn't brought in those key people at the stages that we did.

—**Cassandra Curtis, cofounder of Once Upon a Farm**

All that said . . .

In this instance, it doesn't work. The company gets too top-heavy. The head count is too much to support the expense and you have to lay people off. They didn't justify the expense and now you are looking at more limited funds. Now you have to reconsider how to use what's left. You can increase your marketing in the hopes that it will increase your sales, or you can lower your cost to stay in business.

To **lower your costs**, turn to page 143

To **invest in marketing**, turn to page 147

The term "profit and loss" (P&L) is a common one in any business. Do you spend less than you earn? After you hired a big team that you couldn't afford, you have to get out of the hole so you can maintain operations with cash flow.

In the CPG business, your two key metrics are margin and consumption. How much money do you have left after you spend everything you need to spend, and how frequently are people purchasing your product. Most likely when you started this company, you weren't thinking about scale, operational efficiencies, production timelines, and cost of goods. It was all about the integrity of the product.

At this point, you're paying for that short-sightedness. Now all you can look at is your bottom line. You keep asking yourself what's necessary. You start examining your operations and making things more efficient. How can you reduce the overhead and increase your margins? Are we paying people to do jobs that are not providing a return?

You pick apart the operations, from how you pack your boxes, to what materials you use, to the size of the boxes. Sometimes you can save money on shipping just by changing the box dimensions. For instance, postal delivery service charges less for certain shapes and sizes of boxes.

You scrutinize the way you're producing your goods. What inefficiencies are happening in the production line? Why are you making three or four flavors when only one sells? You can find better agreements and get better contracts in place. You can build your own facility. You can even find a different recipe formulation with some compromises. You see that one of your agreements is crazy expensive to source a specific ingredient and there's an equally healthy alternative that's far less expensive.

As you start to look closely at how to grow your company, you'll understand how to manage your cash needs through operational efficiencies. You can get the company really dialed in to where you can grow in a hyperefficient manner. But if you keep cutting costs, at some point your quality will get compromised and the taste of the product will change.

I am constantly, almost weekly, reevaluating the team and the budgets to determine what is going to keep us solvent in the next thirteen weeks. As of the writing of this book, I had to cut my team by half, including friends and people who were doing good work, but it wasn't mission-critical work. We aren't able to do everything we want, but we are doing what we have to. I wake up every morning and ask what three things have to go right that day. Everything else can fall away. It's just noise. I just focus on those three things.

All that said . . .

You can only cut costs so much. There is still a cash-flow problem that can only be remedied by selling more product to turn a profit. If you're not careful, all of a sudden, you'll put yourself out of business. You have to sell, and you have to sell fast.

To **invest in marketing**, turn to page 147

As Veronica, you have different needs and constraints than Nathaniel, who also considered building a facility. You've taken professional money from professional investors. It could be a VC, private equity, any number of different investment funds or groups of funders or wealthy individuals. At this point, though, no matter who they are, they are expecting a return. That is your job. You have to get a return on their investment and do it within a window of time. That is going to start constraining your choices.

Buying assets to build facilities is not an option if you want the biggest return on investment. Most investors want to see sales and marketing increases. They want the brand to build, build, build. Their thinking is: "Why are you going to build a facility if you're going to sell to a conglomerate in a couple years that has its own facilities?" Big food conglomerates don't buy facilities, they buy brands.

Your biggest bang for the buck if you are an investor is to build brands. Building brands requires sales and marketing. So while you, as a founder, might have a desire to control your destiny in building your facility to maintain your food quality, it really doesn't fit the window that an investor needs for the timeline they have. They often say it takes twice as long and twice as much to build out a facility when those dollars could be used instead to drive sales and build the brand and take over shelf space and open up more retail accounts.

That's where the money goes. You chose this path for the right reasons, but really you've taken a fork in the road that is going to start driving your decisions as you build a brand instead of a business.

All that said . . .

You really don't have this choice. You took a fork in the road when you accepted the professional money. The clock is ticking, and the brand has to be built. Not a facility. There is a clearly defined path for you now, with only one way in and one way out.

To **invest in marketing**, turn to page 147

Nick Saltarelli from Mid-Day Squares said, "The first hypothesis of every food company should be: Are random people willing to pay you for your product? We didn't even think about expanding manufacturing until we could prove to ourselves that we could sell $250,000 worth of bars in our first twelve months."

Most investors don't want equipment. They don't want infrastructure. They want to show growth, and the quickest way to grow is to aggressively market your product.

Investors really want things like Super Bowl commercials. This suits their desire for hypergrowth. If you're lucky, you can have strong growth and high profitability, but that doesn't happen very often. Most of the time it's strong growth and very low profitability because you're reinvesting any profits back into growth. In fact, you're given grief if you don't plow every bit of profit and then some back into growth.

With consumer goods, you have to produce the product before you can sell it. The faster you grow, the more inventory you need, which means the more cash you need to produce the inventory. And sometimes when you're selling to a big retailer, that sixty-day waiting period can get you into trouble. It might be three months from when you first started production to get paid. The bigger the retailers, the bigger the cash demands.

But marketing is really important because when sales are increasing, even if your margins are razor thin and getting thinner, good marketing is still lifting everything. When times are good, when you're making hay, a lot of problems don't come to the surface. You can glide over the inefficiencies. When things are going great, nobody cares. It's like the best ride in the world. But one little hiccup and all of a sudden, the cracks start to show. People start to complain. Things begin to fall apart. And a lot of other things get forgotten or mismanaged in that process.

When you take venture capital, you may not have time to address any of these problems. There's an end game you have to aim for, and that's an exit. When I say exit, I mean being acquired by a major company or listing an IPO. There is a lot riding on your success, and so your stress levels are pretty much always high. But you have chosen to take the ride because you want to create this challenger to these huge incumbent established brands or pantry staples.

> We knew we wanted to build a strong brand. Investors said we needed to grow the top line and it was OK to lose money to be able to sell the company down the line. But for us, it was not about just growing our top line with OK margins. We wanted to have a healthy, sustainable company AND be the leader within the category. CPG can be so cash consuming. You kind of get on a hamster wheel of fundraising if you aren't careful.
>
> **—Vanessa Dew, cofounder of Health-Ade**

You chose to invest your cash predominantly in marketing because you believe marketing will increase sales, leading to more retail accounts, more shelf space, and ultimately more consumption from customers. It costs money to get into stores. Now you might be paying more than you should for those customers, but it's still just getting that behavior set, so you justify it.

Marketing is your rocket fuel.

All that said . . .

Sales increase. You're opening new accounts. But to get them, you're spending a lot of promotional dollars and because of this, your margins begin to erode. So now the decision needs to be made: Do you focus on building your retail or do you pull back and focus on marketing directly to the customer using the internet?

Decision: Do you focus on direct-to-consumer sales or retail?

To **focus on direct-to-consumer sales**, turn to page 150

To **focus on retail**, turn to page 156

You Focus on Direct-to-Consumer Sales

Direct-to-consumer (DTC) e-commerce is very responsive. When you make one change, you can see an increase or decrease in sales nearly overnight.

This method is great because in a way, you can go back to the trial-and-error days you experienced at the beginning. You can try different package sizes and pricing and marketing. You can tinker with words and images. It's just an infinitely flexible, adaptable, and responsive sales channel. You can really find your voice while you find your audience.

It's exciting. You actually own the customer relationship. You know who your customer is. You can put them on subscriptions. Once you get somebody to buy a second time, you don't have to market to them again. You know your best new customers as well as your existing customers. You know them by name; you can market new products to them. It becomes a very valuable relationship.

E-commerce is incredibly attractive because you can gather so much data. You know you've spent a certain amount of marketing dollars to get specific customers in the door. And now they're buying from you every month; they're subscribers. You can measure those profits and losses pretty easily.

Another advantage of direct-to-consumer marketing is that it is great for cash flow. You get paid almost immediately.

In my experience with DTC, it can be very intoxicating. You think it's the way to make a tremendous profit. But it's actually extremely volatile. I still see retail as the more stable approach and DTC as a smaller piece. It's hard to turn it away because it seems to make sense. Until it doesn't.

As quick as that money comes in, it can literally go away overnight. Think of how spending will shift when there is a disaster. Or how fads rise up and fade away inexplicably. So many things influence the way people spend their money, from elections to holidays to global pandemics. It's impossible to predict these fluctuations.

A friend's company was doing $60 million in DTC revenue and was on track to double that revenue in a year. For certain reasons, their social media ad accounts got flagged and banned overnight and drove their revenue to zero. They had to scramble to survive that year, and it took everything they could do just to stay afloat.

Another challenge that exists right now is that there are only two or three major advertising platforms on the internet. When any one of those changes a term or a policy, you could just be shut off. You can also be shut off because, for some reason, it glitches—maybe one online marketing platform thinks you made a claim that they don't like or there is some willy-nilly glitch in the system.

All of a sudden, your storefront is gone and you have to fight to get it up and running again. You can't get an answer from the robots who supposedly field emails. Good luck trying to contact a human. Weeks go by and you can't do much more than just sit there waiting for them to figure out the problem. You're at their mercy.

You have to consider the cost as well. Advertising on the internet is basically an auction. You're bidding for eyeballs. If there are other bidders willing to spend more, you don't get your ads. Nobody sees your product because somebody else bid more for your customer. That's the online marketplace. You're beholden to the dynamics of those major platforms you're advertising on, and things can change in the blink of an eye.

So the best practice is to make online marketing only a portion of your marketing and sales strategy. But it's really hard to diversify when things are going great. You may be making six to ten times every dollar on those e-commerce ads. If you were to spend that same dollar elsewhere, it wouldn't generate as much income. So there's an opportunity cost. It's really hard to say, "Hey, everyone, let's spend the money somewhere else that isn't as profitable."

All that said . . .

That day arrives when everything comes crashing down. You are left wondering what just happened. How did you go from $10,000 to $15,000 a day down to $500? You don't know what's going on! Sales just stop and it's completely out of your control. So now you either have to try to diversify your sales and marketing into other online channels or move back into retail.

Decision: Do you diversify online sales or move to retail?

To **diversify online sales**, turn to page 153

To **focus on retail**, turn to page 156

I can personally say when you have more than one or two sales channels, your stress levels drastically decrease. When there is a glitch or something goes wrong, you can still function because all your berries are not in one basket. I, personally, am better able to perform when there is more than one revenue stream.

Diversifying is tough, though, because now that you have been cut off at the knees, you don't have that dependable profit coming in. You are gun-shy about investing in marketing, so you want to be prudent.

Well, all those sparkly ads you invested in are not performing anymore and you're feeling pretty down. You're at this point where you've gotten high on your own supply, like a drug dealer. You got hooked on the success of your platform. But now that platform is not giving you the high it was before, and you feel lost.

It takes time to ramp up and build momentum in any type of new sales channel. Once you have that momentum, it's going to be another wait to see any measurable impact or income. You find yourself stuck. You cannot perform the way you want to financially as you ramp up the new channels. You don't have any sort of insulation to absorb another loss.

So you go back to your operations and lower the cost of your product to increase the volume. But instead of just coming out and saying you've lowered the price, you offer discounts and incentives to spur purchases. You know what I'm talking about. If someone abandons their cart on the web, you give them 20 percent off the next order. If they come back the next day, you start offering incentives to chase that sale.

You start to get desperate. You wonder if you should send an email to every single one of your customers. Give them 10 percent off today just to get the money in the door. But in the back of your head, you know that's not a really good sales tactic.

So you start thinking you'll just lower the price completely. You'll offer free shipping too. At this point, you are obviously just giving away things to see how you can get a dollar in the door. And at the end of the day, you don't like your margins.

You're digging a bigger hole. You might get a sale, but that sale doesn't even cover the cost of the product you produced because you've spent money to market it. You start looking at how everything adds up. You just spent $100 to sell $30 worth of product. That doesn't work for more than a couple of weeks.

All that said . . .

You're done. This ending doesn't happen overnight. It usually takes several weeks or months. You already know the writing is on the wall, but you don't want to give up because it's become a passion.

You can't help thinking back to when you did have sales. You can't let go. It's become something you have to fix. You have a team of people here, but you can't pay them. So you begin letting them go.

You start to really pay attention to what's mission critical. A lot of the flashy marketing stuff is unnecessary. You just focus on sales, because without sales, you can't do anything. And that's what puts you in the trap. As you've been making all these last-ditch efforts in an attempt to right the ship, you didn't actually lighten the load. It's panic mode for a couple of weeks until something gives.

You desperately clutch at ideas. Maybe you can go to retail! But retail is going to look at your product and say, "I can buy it online for X dollars but you're charging me more." So now you offer them another 50 percent off. And you just can't sustain yourself at all.

You've cut your price so low that with that 50 percent margin, there's no room for any profit. By cutting costs, you run yourself into bankruptcy. You sell out of whatever inventory you have left, and you shut down.

Or maybe you can't even do that. There is no return to your investors, and you have to just walk away.

THE
END

You Focus on Retail

You get a big chain interested, and they place a big order. This is your opportunity to really make it.

On the retail route, your sales are growing. The margins are smaller, but you're staying profitable, and then this order comes in. You're lucky because you priced your product high enough to make it work. (If you missed the discussion about how to price your product, go to the decision on page 36, "Do you price your product for profit or price at a comparable rate?")

How do you fulfill the order? You are already in local and regional retailers and you have an online profile that is growing as well. You set your price to make a healthy margin, which should work in retail to give everybody that percentage of profit that they need to touch, handle, move, or display the product.

But you suddenly have two hundred stores to stock. It's an incredibly exciting and humbling moment. For the first time, you really feel like this is the big leagues. Nobody wants to say no at this point. Business owners will try to make it work at this stage, knowing it can fall apart in the negotiations, but I think nearly everyone accepts that first invitation.

So you take the retailer meeting and you are able to secure this deal. And now you have a big decision before you, because you have to figure out how to fulfill the order. The reality is that you can only produce so much product. How do you physically manufacture so much? How do you cover the cost of manufacturing, and how do you transport it to the retailer? How do you market it once it's in the retailer?

All that said . . .

You have to decide if you're going to stop selling your product to other customers so that you have enough to fulfill the order. Or you can raise money again for a third round of funding.

Decision: Do you stop selling or raise more money?

To **stop selling**, turn to page 158

To **raise more money**, turn to page 160

You Stop Selling

You have to pull out of existing relationships.

With a bigger account coming on board, you have to reallocate resources and maybe stop selling to your underperforming clients. Maybe you don't have to be in certain coffee shops. You can stop selling to your online retailers and resellers.

You rally all the focus around this one big order to make this work. You figure if this is the big leagues, you have to do it right. You have a finite amount of resources, so you have to shunt them; you have to pull a resource, a body, a brain off other tasks and put them on this new retailer. You focus everyone on the team on this one goal.

When you launch in this retailer, you need to drive your customers there to ensure that this product is going to move off shelves. Maybe you redirect some of your people who are doing social media posts to work on figuring out how to support this launch.

Because that retail launch is the priority at this point, you're going to lose sales elsewhere. You're going to make yourself fully dependent on that one channel. In the back of your head, you know when you are fully consolidated in one place, you could get knocked sideways, just like you can with direct-to-consumer sales.

But you are fully invested, so you take a small team and do your best to get it into the stores. It's not nearby. You're based in San Diego and they'll launch in Chicago.

All that said . . .

What you fear will happen does happen. The product simply doesn't move off the shelves. It could be a communication issue. It could be product market fit. It could be that customers don't want to spend the money you're charging. It could be any number of reasons.

But the fact of the matter is that the retailer does not repurchase. You put all your berries in one basket and unfortunately it was not worth the gamble. You run out of money. The retailer returns the product, and you're on the brink of going out of business.

Now everyone who works for you is out of a job if you don't raise money again. And fast.

To **raise more money**, turn to page 160

You Raise More Money

This is your third round of raising money. Remember that with every round of investments comes dilution. Now you're down to owning less than 50 percent of your company. And only 30 percent of companies are even able to raise a third round.

But here you are, raising more money. Damn the demand, it just keeps coming. More retailers want more product; there are more and more inventory needs; you need more and more staff to support your growth. It's exciting and terrifying all at once. You made your decision to go big, so you're buckled up. This is your moon-shot moment, if you will.

Because of the success today, you're feeling unstoppable. Publicly your brand is a darling. But somehow there's still an inkling in your head that this feels a little precarious—and it is. You should have some doubts. You should be thinking more about how many people you are bringing on. What happens if this doesn't get sold? What's your personal obligation? How much money are you going to have to return if this fizzles instead of becoming an explosion of success?

These are all rational thoughts when you're going back for subsequent fundraising rounds, but most importantly, you should truly consider if you're 100 percent committed to the life of endless fundraising.

Thankfully you were smart. Before your company started spinning out of control, you worried that something could go terribly wrong with your retailer. So, before it did, you used that picture of success to get new investors. You told them you needed the money so that you could execute flawlessly on this retail launch. And you were able to secure the funds in exchange for a hefty chunk of ownership.

The moment you own less than half of your company, it's a shock. You realize that your company has gone from a passion to nothing more than a vehicle for generating investor returns, which now includes yourself as an investor. It becomes a financial instrument.

But that can't matter now. You tell your investors that you are planning to go into other retailers and that will consume cash. You make a plan to max out marketing and staffing to ensure success.

You bounce back and see the rocket-ship growth. But as your ownership dwindles, you have less chance of exiting. This is because the more money you take in, the more money has to be returned. If you bring in a billion dollars, you have to return a billion plus. That's a huge difference from taking in a hundred dollars. The more money your company generates, the less the chance you can fail and just walk away. You get stuck on a hamster wheel.

Everyone's gunning for that big exit at this stage of growth. You are preparing to sell your company to another company. But here's the thing about an acquisition: the bigger you get, the less likely you are to be acquired.

It means the purchase price gets larger, and there are only so many companies that can cut these big checks. How many major food companies are willing to pay a billion dollars for a young food company, no matter how successful it is? The pyramid gets smaller at the top.

The other irony in food is that there are restrictions on who can buy you. Oddly enough, a food company can buy a tech company, but a tech company can't buy a food company. The infrastructure is not there. There are a finite set of buyers in food because of the perishability and the supply chain. Not many companies can absorb a big acquisition like that.

All that said . . .

You are past that point of no return. The only choice you have left is to either continue to raise money because you have to grow or stall growth.

But stalling growth is not an option because you own less than 50 percent of your company now. You have a board and other investors. They want to maximize their returns. If you try to suggest that you're not going to grow the company, you are actually violating your fiduciary responsibility to investors, and you can get fired from your own company, which happens frequently. Then they bring in professional CEOs whose job is to grow the wheels off the company and make it look pretty and put a bow on it for somebody else to buy it or to take an IPO. Quality be damned.

To **raise even more money**, turn to page 163

So if you haven't figured this out yet, this is no longer a company. Rather, it is a financial instrument focused on generating returns. You are no longer in control of what happens because you own less than 30 percent. The only choice you have left is to continue to grow. And your chance of an exit now is 6 percent.

The more you grow, the more money you consume. The more money you raise, the more accounts you get. New accounts can take a long time and require a lot of marketing support (AKA costs) to execute well, so you may be looking at negative profits at the beginning.

Your brand is recognizable, and there are little ego strokes everywhere when people find out it's your company. But financially, it is a house of cards. You're giving away free product all the time so people can sample things in the hopes that they'll get hooked. But they don't get hooked on your product. They just take the free samples because people love free things. If you were to turn off the marketing dollars, the existing sales go away, which means your overhead is too big.

You're looking for a buyer. You hope that a big food conglomerate will come in. If they do, they will say, "We can make this thing profitable real quick." That's the thinking of a buyer. They'll put in a whole lot of money and pull out a lot of the operational costs. They will take it much bigger than you ever could.

All that said . . .

A buyer doesn't show up.

Decision: Do you shut down or raise even more money?

To **shut down**, turn to page 165

To **raise even more money**, turn to page 166

You didn't time it right. Few do.

This could be for a number of reasons. Maybe it's a global pandemic, and nobody wants to invest in anything for six months. Or maybe all of a sudden your particular food goes out of vogue and investors flee. They migrate away from you like locusts and take the resources with them. Or maybe the big companies only make two major acquisitions a year and both have already been signed this year, so they're not buying anymore.

There are a million reasons why 1 to 2 percent of companies ever really exit. Don't take it too hard. There's always another idea out there. Maybe this is a sign that it's time to chase the next dream.

THE
END

You Raise Even More Money

Buckle up, buttercup. You are on your way to being a global brand.

All the stars have aligned. You want to take this thing to the moon, and once you get there, you're not coming back. Anyone who has raised significant sums of money like this has entered a zero-sum game. You're in it to win it. You wanted to build that global behemoth, that challenger brand, and you've done it.

The huge buyers have appeared, and it will take several months to figure out all the details now. The complexity of these transactions is astounding. At this stage, you own only 10 percent of your company and your chance of exit is 2 percent. Only 9 percent of companies ever raise a fifth round.

Everyone knows at any point it could all go away. Anything can happen and change the deal. A natural disaster. A political upheaval. A major strike somewhere along the supply chain. A wobble in the economy. Even a global pandemic!

It might happen the day before selling, and suddenly everything changes or goes on hold. You have to go back to the investors' table, and they ask to see your recent numbers. You're like, "Whoa, whoa! Something major just happened." But they don't care. They want to see new numbers.

The whole world comes to a stop, and you probably come to a stop with it. But they look at your numbers and say, "Hmm, they are not as good as they were before. We're going to change the price."

You wonder what kind of world you are living in. You have to ride things right to the line. Everyone's trying to get the best deal for themselves. It's exhausting and fatiguing.

You've taken all these rounds of capital, and now there's a thing called "liquidity preference," which is a bit of a nuanced term. It means the investors in each round you raised get their money out in the order in which they invested (i.e., last money in, first money out), and they take anywhere from 1x to 2x their investment out for each round. This is because of what's called a "waterfall." The way the deals are done and how much money comes out before the next person gets theirs makes the numbers do weird things. By the time it gets to the founder it's far less than you expect. The average founder in the fifth round owns 11 to 12 percent of their company at exit, which is tiny. But to make matters worse, they only see about 6 percent of the transaction. Let's pretend you own 10 percent of your company and your company sells for $100 million. You're really only going to see about six million of that, even though you own 10 percent.

Once you reach the stage of acquisition or IPO, you no longer own the company. You may be the founder in name, but really, you're just another name.

After you are acquired, you typically have to go work for the acquiring company for three to five years to get your money out. They bought your company, and for you to get your full money out (that 6 percent you have left), you have an "earn out." This means they'll give you a chunk of change up front, and getting the remainder of it is actually based on future company performance. Remember, this is a company you no longer really control.

Through all the marketing and the glitz and the sheen and the verbiage, it's all there to support the financial returns of the company and your investors. You sit on a board and have to listen to their decisions to compromise over profitability or growth. But you don't have any other choice because when you take this many rounds of investment, you're on a binary path. It's bankruptcy or get acquired. In some rare cases you might get listed on the public stock exchange, but the chances of that happening are beyond rare.

So you put your head down, show up to work every day, and think wistfully back to those days when you were dreaming big and sincerely considering eating your dog's food because your bank account was that low.

Charles's
PATH

You Are Now Charles

You have an inherent desire to create something of permanence, to create a legacy, something that has true, measurable impact. This is why you started Truth in Cacao. You are aware that this will take a much longer route, and you're OK with that. If it takes decades to achieve the kind of change you are seeking, you won't mind.

What's tough is that you still have to work within the confines of an industry. You still have to interact with retailers and brokers and distributors. You know you have to pick your battles sometimes. Your task is to pick whether to push on all fronts or to push on one front and compromise a little bit on others. It could be margin or use of distributors, for example.

You expect the journey to be long and hard because ideals don't always fit the marketplace. You know you won't have a choice—to some degree you need to function in a certain way within the marketplace to get your product to grocery stores. There are pretty standard ways of doing things when it comes to who gets involved, what those people charge, and what you're expected to do once you get to retail. You're not an exception. Yet.

For now, your cacao is just another item on the shelf for a retailer, but you are on a mission to change that. You are going in with a David versus Goliath mentality, which to a certain degree is healthy. But to another degree, it's going to be tough to get your product to market. If you don't ever get on the shelves because you won't compromise on quality or margin or marketing, you don't stand a chance at changing the food industry or the commodity class. You'll never get to actually deliver on the promise of your goal.

You may think that you don't have to abide by the rules of the marketplace. You are in the business of giving back. There are a lot of founders who think like that in the beginning. But you are seasoned enough to know that a business has to generate profits before it can do anything. At the end of the day, you have to be a functioning company to even contemplate giving back.

Before you begin, you have to decide what kind of company you want.

Decision: Do you want to build a company for permanence or for quick exit?

To **choose a quick exit**, turn to page 171

To **build for permanence**, turn to page 172

False choice! You would never do that.

To **build for permanence**, turn to page 172

(And I hope you turned to this page just because you were curious.)

You Build for Permanence

A company of permanence must have profitability.

I have personally managed a venture fund. I was part of the problem I see around food consolidation. Yes, we may have sold our company to a bigger company, but that is not my passion. I get no energy from that. It began to weigh heavily on my mind that it was a synthetic, cheap win without substance or legacy. To take an alternative path and create a company with permanence resonates off the charts with me.

A lot of times it means profitability at the expense of growth. It is a slower route because you're building something that's stable. It means saying no a lot. It is a whole different type of decision-making because you're not thinking about the next quarter or even the next year. You're making decisions that are, you know, ten, fifteen, twenty years out.

You need to be careful not to take the bait. You say no to a big retailer who comes to you because you don't want to put strain on your supply chain. Instead, you invest in that supply chain, establishing direct relationships with your producers. These are things that investors will say don't make financial sense if you're thinking on the five-year horizon. But you do it anyway because it makes complete sense when you're thinking twenty or fifty years out.

To create permanence means to build a company that is making real social change, a company that focuses on quality of the supply chain, quality of the product, and quality of relationships.

What does it take to be an iconoclast? It takes conviction. It takes resilience. It takes perseverance. It takes vision. It takes self-control.

It's all sacrifice. You're going to lose personal relationships. You're not going to get what you want a lot of the time, and you're going to make do with what you have, but you know it's a worthwhile endeavor. You focus on leadership and stewardship.

You can't let the fox in the henhouse with your finances. You will only accept money from people who love what you're doing and believe in your product. You have to steer clear of certain types of investors. Taking as much money as you could ever imagine sounds great, but then their agenda and your agenda can potentially be grossly misaligned.

All that said . . .

The biggest concern at this point, now that you've decided to build a business based on permanence, is sourcing. You know you have to source the highest-quality product, and if that is the case, you have to start looking overseas because cacao isn't grown in the United States, at least not at the scale you need. Knowing this, do you prefer to use existing brokers and importers to be the go-between as you get on your feet, or do you want to build relationships with producers overseas on your own?

Decision: Do you build relationships with producers or do you use existing brokers and importers?

To **work with existing brokers and importers**, turn to page 174

To **build relationships with producers**, turn to page 176

You Work with Existing Brokers and Importers

The complexities of having your source overseas is daunting at first, so you decide to do whatever you can with those existing brokers and importers. You know they are part of the problem you are trying to solve, but you're going to try it anyway. You need a start.

It's hard to get their attention because you have no track record. You're a small fry so they ignore you. Once you do get their attention, it's hard to impart your standards on their practices.

You're here in the United States, and you're trying to source cacao from Ghana. There are export groups, but those are also the groups that are the antithesis of what you want. You go to them and say, "I want to buy a small amount, but it has to be with higher standards," and they laugh at you.

It's next to impossible to communicate to them the altruistic, better labor and sourcing practices you want to see. And it will be impossible to communicate that to the customer when you're using the same people that have those bad practices you are decrying. But they offer to partner with you, making it clear they aren't going to change the way they do things.

All that said . . .

They're not going to conform to your cause because you're not a big enough buyer. Now you face a conundrum. Do you lower your standards just to get the product rolling? Take what is best today and work for a better tomorrow? Or do you say no and hold fast to your mission so that you don't become part of the problem?

Decision: Do you lower your standards or work directly with producers?

To **build relationships with producers**, turn to page 176

To **lower your standards**, turn to page 180

You Build Relationships with Producers

Since you turned down the partnership with the brokers and import-ers, you have no other option than to build relationships with pro-ducers by yourself.

First, you have to find producers. You get on a plane to Ghana with very little information, and you might have one or two contacts, and you spend two or three weeks there meeting with people. It's a slow process. You are backpacking and busing around bumpy dirt roads and sleeping under mosquito nets.

You luck out and find a really small co-op of producers that grow high-quality cacao and are operating in conditions you want to sup-port. But they can't produce at scale. You don't mind—you would rather take the higher quality at a much smaller scale and help them build. But who's going to get it out of the country?

You try to figure out how to ship the cacao once it's ready. You'll have to meet with ministries of trade and agriculture and commerce before you leave the country. They'll usually have somebody who will know how to export the cacao, but you have to be careful. Remember those brokers and importers? They have longer-standing relation-ships than you do and they don't want you to succeed. Not to mention bribes are very real in this world. They could be paying off somebody in the ministries if they don't want them to approve your export.

It's a bit of a cloak-and-dagger effort. You just have to hope that your competitors don't catch wind that you are here until all the paperwork is filed. It can get very combative when you're working with a global commodity class. If you are noticeable—if you start to make noise or get to a size that's perceived as threatening—you're going to come under attack from those who want you to fail.

What would you do then? Go get the cacao every harvest and bring it home in your suitcase? Smuggle it out of the country and hope you have enough to make a production run and also hope it doesn't get confiscated going through customs? That's ridiculous. You'd never do that. Forget it.

All that said . . .

But you are full of ingenuity and just enough audacity to succeed. You find your source, you secure the export agreements, and you nail down shipping, so you are all set to receive your first delivery as soon as the producers have it ready.

You've spent a lot of money on travel expenses to this point, but you know that processing is going to take a lot more money. You have to decide if you want to continue to operate from the money that is coming in or find another source of capital. You can pitch to small, committed investors who would act as altruistic partners and see if they will support your vision. Or you can fund operations through your cash flow.

Decision: Do you operate from cash flow or pitch to investors?

To **operate from cash flow**, turn to page 178

To **pitch to investors**, turn to page 181

You Operate from Cash flow

When you make a decision to operate from cash flow, you have to be hyperfocused on what you can do with the resources you have. There are an infinite number of things you could do, and perhaps even should do, but you can't do them because you're constrained in both capital and time.

This choice leads to a vigorous prioritization, which is really challenging because you might have opportunities present themselves that seem to be once in a lifetime, but you have to pass on them. Getting comfortable with missing opportunities that you really want is tough, but it's required when you make the decision to limit yourself to your company's cash flow.

You're going to feel like you're always stealing from Peter to pay Paul. You will have days like I have, where I get a purchase order for $26,000, and right after that, I get an unexpected invoice for $27,000. Within a matter of minutes, I'm negative $1,000. That happens frequently. There's always something coming in and something going out.

You'll have advisors and investors and service providers and vendors and marketers (always marketers) who find you with some whizbang idea that they want to sell you. Or there is something that you need to fix because a customer complained about a package. Get comfortable saying, "We can't do that today," and "We'll have to cross that bridge when we can," and "We'll have to do that later, when we can afford it." Phrases like this become like a silent mantra for every consideration you have. Every single decision gets run through this.

With Pass the Honey, there have been countless times when we've only had so much inventory and we've had to tell a vendor or a new wholesale account that we could not fulfill their purchase order. We need to have the cash flow, but we also want to have enough inventory so we can sell directly to the consumer because that's where we make better margins. It can be a knife's-edge balancing act. However, with all that said, I've been able to retain more ownership with this approach. It isn't the easy route, that's certain. Until you can get peace with all the tension, it's incredibly stressful.

All that said . . .

Just know you're going to be moving slower than if you take outside money. You're not going to maximize every opportunity. You're going to pick up the less-is-more mentality. However, you do know you can still move forward. You can lower your standards to keep things more manageable or you can pitch to investors and try to raise some more money to achieve your idealistic standards.

Decision: Do you lower your standards or pitch to investors?

To **lower your standards**, turn to page 180

To **pitch to investors**, turn to page 181

You Lower Your Standards

False choice!

You wouldn't do that. You began this company with a very specific cause in mind, so that choice is not on the table for you.

To **pitch to investors,** turn to page 181

It's ironic that sometimes it's easier to raise money when you don't have a product than when you do because you're raising money for a vision. People get behind a vision.

Your decision is to find those right investors. But keep in mind that the chances of getting funding at this point are 50/50 at best.

Here's the funny thing. It's almost more difficult to raise money after you have a bit of success than it is with nothing at all. If you have a product with actual measurable results, good or bad, you're going to get penalized somehow because it didn't meet someone's expectation—you're not going to land right with somebody. They're either going to expect the price to be higher or lower or the packaging to be different or the sales to go another way.

But right now you just have a vision. Couple that with your strong purpose, and what you're really doing is looking for ambassadors. These aren't venture capitalists. Rather, they are impact investors. These are investors who aren't looking to maximize their financial returns as much as they're looking at ecological returns, social concerns, and other worthy societal causes.

These investors are not looking to squeeze every dollar out of an investment, but they do want to know that there are ancillary benefits. There is a triple bottom line consideration.

They are fewer and far between, so finding them is going to take some time. By nature, these are private individuals with a lot of money. They're intentionally hidden. You have to know where to look and how to appeal to what matters to them. Your personal and professional connections will make all the difference here. They don't publicize a lot.

The wealthiest families in America all have private family offices that do investments, but you're not going to see a big glorious website about them. It's word of mouth.

Or, if you're really new, you can go to impact investment summits. You can join associations for companies doing "evergreen" work, as it is often called. That is how I've found most of our evergreen investors. When you find investors for a purpose-driven company, alignment of interest and passion is key.

Impact investors are risk averse. You have to get a certain amount of traction under your belt or have a big enough vision in the beginning to get their attention. They want to make sure that they're going to put a dollar in, and while it may not get maximum return, it's going to be less risky. There's a risk-return ratio that you have to strike.

Obviously this process takes much longer. The metrics of success are very different. You're going to handle smaller checks and more investors. Your narrative must be developed to the point where people understand what you do. You have to get really good at telling people what it is that you're doing with a story that is polished and ready to tell any time.

Part of that narrative is to help people see that it's not a crazy pie-in-the-sky idea. It is tangible and it will be executed. Shoot for executable and explainable.

You can be pretty certain big money isn't going to come for a long time. Your investors are not going to risk a ton, but they really like what you're doing. They like you. As the company matures, you get bigger and bigger checks. By the time you are four years in, you're finally seeing ten-, fifteen-, twenty-, and thirty-million-dollar revenue, and all of a sudden, the bigger checks start to show up. But you have to get established. You have a track record, a history. You need to be a known entity who is doing really good work and hasn't compromised. This is something to look forward to, but it takes a long time.

Let me get a little "woo-woo" here. I have given up my power to others far too frequently, and many times that happened in investor meetings where I thought I had to defend decisions and answer every question they posed. They aren't the experts on your company. Yes, you have to describe and explain, but just because someone has money does not mean that they are right. The feeling of panhandling or the "song and dance" or "dog and pony show" are common phrases because that's how it feels. It's a power dynamic that is icky for me. It took me a while to realize I was the best person to speak for my company.

I knew it better than anyone else. I did not need to contort my ideas and the way I run my company to fit the ideas of an investor. The best investors I've found are when it's a dialogue, not a pitch. The very word "pitch" irritates me. I'll tell you what I'm doing, and if you like it, you like it, and if you don't, you don't. With the honeycomb business, there were a lot of naysayers. But in this case, I've been on the winning side. That wasn't always the case. Maybe that's what comes with age? Dare I say I'm gaining some measure of wisdom?

All that said . . .

So, back to the matter at hand. You have your really great co-op of producers. And you worked really hard, and now you have enough capital to start producing your first round of product. The decision placed before you is, Where are you going to produce? Will you go with a co-packer or not?

Decision: Are you going to find a co-packer or build your own facility?

To **find a co-packer**, turn to page 185

To **build your own facility**, turn to page 186

False choice!

You can't go with a co-packer because you require higher quality controls and you can't break the chain of custody. To achieve your mission, control of your product is absolutely vital.

Quality and accountability are your tent poles. You can't just hand them off to somebody who's making a product with garbage for a different brand. It doesn't fit the script. You've chosen this path of fierce independence and authenticity and accountability and transparency.

You have to build your own facility to maintain your standards, which means you need more money.

To **build your own facility**, turn to page 186

You Build Your Own Facility

You are true to your vision of a pure product that upends the practices that have become acceptable. Legacy companies tend to build their own facility a little farther down the road in their journey. Building your own facility is one very good way to maintain control and standards. Unlike a company that's venture backed, for companies looking for permanence and legacy, this step will usually take five years or more.

(Note: If you haven't already read the story of building a facility and you want to learn about this now, go back and read the "You Build Your Own Facility" choice on page 97.)

All that said . . .

To build your own facility, you need money.

To **find impact investors**, turn to page 187

You can't go with venture capital, so you go back to your impact investors and ask for more.

You knew when you made the decision to run a company that stands on its own, it came with many trade-offs. I've done it both ways. There's the frustration that comes when you know your product is good. And then you watch a competitor go raise what seems to be effortless, endless capital, and you ask yourself why. Their product sucks. Their branding sucks. It's no different from all the other soul-suckingly boring products out there. How are they able to raise nine, ten, thirty million dollars when here you are struggling to make do with something so far superior?

The status quo cannot be trusted. It is impossible to produce in the time frames that investors expect. You can't possibly tackle fair trade and social justice in three to five years.

Not to mention that you will have a conflict of interest. Their desire is to generate profit and growth over the shortest amount of time. Both of these will compromise your ability to source the highest-quality ingredients and invest thoughtfully in your supply chain.

Most investors will never get behind putting dollars into your supply chain at the levels you want. They don't justify it as a meaningful use of funds. In their mind, you should always be investing in marketing, grow, grow, grow, and never do anything that doesn't drive a sale. That is the worst side of venture capital. Of course, they are not all that way, but some are, so I'm giving you the worst of the worst. If you were to cave and go with venture capital, you can't build a facility because they don't want the assets. It's cheaper to go with a co-packer and to build a brand that's shallow with a logo on the back of the box or bottle. They just want the brand. They want the customers. It's a shell of a company.

So you go back to your small pool of investors and humbly ask them to help you some more or to refer you to other potential investors.

All that said . . .

You secure more funding and build your facility. Now that you are getting close to manufacturing your product, you have to think through how much you are going to charge for the product. As you know by now, it is going to be high. You are smart enough to know how to price your product for maximum profit margins, but this leads to the next decision.

You have to consider packaging designs. It's really difficult in certain categories, such as cacao, where essentially you're selling powder in a tin can. Do you set your package in a specialized bag, perhaps? Does that bag justify a higher price?

Everything you're doing has to justify a premium position. The consumer has to feel good about their purchase, that they're getting value. It all starts with value in branding. It could be value in convenience. It could be value in quality. It could be value in third-party testing. It could be value from stories of the producers.

There are many ways you can build and show value, and all of them are considered consumer education. Do your customers even know what fair-trade cacao is? Do they know why it is important and what justifies paying a higher price to support it? You have to decide if you want to spend time and money educating consumers about your product, which is more marketing, or if you want to keep spending your money on production.

Decision: Do you keep spending your money on production or do you educate consumers?

To **keep spending on production**, turn to page 190

To **educate the consumer**, turn to page 191

You Keep Spending on Production

False choice!

You have to justify the high cost or nobody will buy your product. Period. You are on the long, hard road of educating consumers through marketing. And by doing so, you are building a loyal customer base.

To **educate the consumer**, turn to page 191

This can be incredibly expensive, and it takes a long time.

You have to educate potential customers about the problem before you can then give them a solution. Cacao is similar to my honeycomb in some respects. People are vaguely aware of the notion of colony collapse. But they don't understand why. They think bees are in danger, but that's the extent of it. I have to educate the public about bees and pollinator habitat before they even think about buying my honeycomb.

When my company started, there weren't a lot of people searching for information on honeycombs. To achieve our aims and purpose, we had to literally pay to interrupt the consumers' social media feeds and capture their attention to explain why they were paying so much more for honeycomb and educate them on the ills of liquid honey. This action took a lot of trial and error and money. More than I expected.

And it isn't just the public you have to educate. You have to educate the retailers and everyone along the supply chain as well. Cassandra Curtis, cofounder of Once Upon a Farm, is one of those rare category creators, and it's been an intense road to get there.

CASE STUDY

Cassandra Curtis

Creating a category is a big deal. In the beginning, there just wasn't space anywhere in the store for fresh baby food like ours. There were no refrigerated sections set out for this, so a lot of retailers were very hesitant because they had never seen anything like it before. There was nothing proven about it yet. It took a lot of pushing to get retailers to try it and to carve out space in their dairy section or put refrigerators in the baby aisle.

We had to go through a whole chain of command to make space for something new in every store we went into, and that takes a lot of time. You have to convince them to either make space on their existing shelves by replacing other products or make space on their floor for your unit. It's a big time commitment.

Now it's pretty much the norm that most stores have a section set out to have refrigerated baby and kids' food, but behind the scenes, this is a big deal. We have to purchase and place the refrigerators, and if they go out, we have to make sure that they get repaired. We have to make sure the stores stock the merchandise correctly because the people working in the baby food section aren't used to merchandising refrigeration. It's a lot.

So, because you are committed to the cause, you educate the public on the problem and then present your product as a solution. You layer this with the quality of your product. You have to educate them again. Not only is it good for the people and the earth, it tastes good. Try it!

Most brands just educate about their product: Look, it's baby food. Now it's baby food in a special jar. Get it? Look, it's candy. Now it's candy in a different flavor. People already understand the category and how it fits into their lives, and you just have to educate on the brand promise. That's something tangible.

But what does a cause look like? What does fair-trade cacao look like? This is partially category creation because you're carving out a subset of an existing category that demands a higher price in the marketplace so that you can actually reinvest in your supply chain to deliver on the promises. That's the whole point of the company.

There is a different type of sales cycle, both digitally and in retail, when you are educating the customer to pay a premium for a familiar product that they didn't even realize had problems.

When you've chosen the route of digital sales, it's very easy to share information. It's not difficult to change and update a website. You can see how your messages resonate and what leads to quicker sales. With that, it's the same story as the others. You get a rich regional interest.

All that said . . .

Interest has been generated and the demand is going up. When demand increases, obviously this is going to take more money. You can stall the growth by throttling back on marketing expenses and risk losing momentum, or you can scramble to meet the demand with more supply. This means traveling again and starting over building relationships with new producers to get more raw ingredients.

> **Decision:** Do you want to stall growth or expand your supply chain to meet the demand?
>
> To **stall growth**, turn to page 194
>
> To **expand to meet the demand**, turn to page 196

You Stall Growth

I stall growth all the time. I pull budgets from DTC, push back on retailers, and try to lower the number of stores we launch in. We don't try to be in every marketplace and every channel. Personally, I think constraints make a better business. Being everywhere all at once is very expensive. I prefer to do a few things very well. This also helps keep the team laser focused. Your investors aren't as stringent as VCs, but they will have some questions about this choice.

Deciding to limit your sales and slow down is a great way to keep the stress low. But it will plateau, forcing you to diversify when performance slips. You have to ramp up other channels, which takes a lot of time.

Many times stalling growth is the best thing for your personal goals. I find that $4 million tends to be the level that a founder can maintain without too much trouble. Many people reach this point and still pretty much run the company from their phone. I wouldn't say effortlessly, but I would say to a large degree, very successfully, without overtly taxing their life and giving them plenty of space to do other things. Typically, with a $4 million company, you don't have another day job.

But some people stall for other reasons. Maybe they are discouraged. Sometimes it's jealousy. Sometimes it's confusion, just watching the marketplace and brands take off that you don't feel are valuable. Choosing a cash-flow route is the longer, harder path, and it wears people out. Raising tons of funds at this stage, as always, has problems.

There are constant trade-offs and compromises that have to be made when you're managing cash. For a while, you have to make do, but that means missteps. And missteps mean you get kicked in the dirt. You've got to stand back up, brush yourself off, and try again. But that is exhausting. How many times do you want to get back up?

All that said . . .

You survive for a while, but eventually your demand dwindles to the point where you can no longer make enough of a profit to continue.

You may end with seven figures annually. But you didn't adhere to your original vision of making a global, sustainable impact and changing an entire commodity class with a company that would survive for generations.

You Expand to Meet the Demand

You turn your focus back to building your supply, which takes time and capital.

You continue to fund your marketing and diversify your channels, but you do not have the sales to cover these expenses.

As you know, you're constantly trying to strike this balance when you're creating a company for longevity. You're always nudging growth a little bit and then managing your operations and supply. And then you're growing the operational side. And then you're back to managing growth.

It's like a little game of inching each one up, but never one too far ahead of the other. You know if you really invest in your supply chain with no education or consumer marketing, you're never going to have enough sales to actually use your supply. But if you push sales too much, your supply chain can't keep up because your quality standards are so high.

So there isn't much choice here. You're continually pushing the bar higher and higher, which means when you get a big account, you can't easily fulfill it. Your supply chain goes up incrementally because your product is different than what's on the global marketplace. You can't place an order for an extra three tons because it doesn't exist.

All that said . . .

When you are faced with big new accounts, you are limited by the very nature of the quality of the supply chain. You're inhibited from growing too fast, but you do want to grow. How else are you going to achieve your vision? You need money to meet the rising demand because sales are only trickling in.

Decision: Do you find more impact investors or try to get a loan?

To **find impact investors**, turn to page 187

To **try to get a loan**, turn to page 198

You Try to Get a Loan

You do your best to find a loan. Unfortunately, you're not considered bankable yet, in terms of a traditional loan. So you have no choice. You just have to go back to the same investors and ask if they have friends who may be interested.

They provide some introductions because those folks usually hang out together. That decision works for nine to twelve months. But eventually you tap out all of those investors.

They've been acting as a bridge; they introduced you to some friends to get you just a little further down the path. And the bridge actually does lead to the opportunity for debt to fund your inventory, which you hope will eventually lead to a banking relationship.

At some point you're just taking whatever comes your way, as long as it's not super predatory. It becomes a blend of equity, convertible notes, short-term debt, vendor financing, anything you're offered. You have all these funky, weird loan structures; some of them are six-month loans and others are three-year loans. Some have interest rates that are higher than others.

You're just trying to get the ball down the field. You can use your steady growth to keep your momentum.

And at a certain point, you have a track record and you are a known entity. Your sales have been consistent, slow but growing. Lo and behold, you are bankable. That's an irony about banks. They don't like fast growth—it's too volatile. They like to see slow, measured, moderate growth with a track record of consistency and less risk.

That's the best way you can get a bank loan. It's not the only way, but it just seems to be the easier, better way.

I think for a purpose-driven company that is growing incrementally over a long period of time, a banking relationship is the linchpin of success. You can take all the loans you had in the past, clean them up in a refinance, and deal with just one lender instead of ten. That makes life a lot easier.

It would also give you the ability to grow knowing that your inventory is going to be covered based on whatever funding comes in the door, which will allow you to free up cash to do marketing. If you need to buy equipment, now you can do that.

You're always trying to free up cash to sink back into educating consumers and increasing product quantities and investing in the supply chain. Very little lending can be used for R&D on a supply chain, but it can be used for inventory purchase orders and equipment and buildings. If you can get those handled by that good banking relationship with some level of peace of mind, you can grow the company reasonably. You're not straining your cash supply.

Obviously the bank takes a cut with their interest rate, but you know, that's doable for the peace of mind.

All that said . . .

For most founders, this isn't an option. They can't raise more money. For you, though, congratulations! You just caught a lucky break. Finally, right?

Now that you have that bankable relationship, you have some money and choices. Do you invest in the supply chain or do you invest in marketing and sales?

Decision: Do you invest in the supply chain or in marketing?

To **invest in the supply chain**, turn to 201

To **invest in marketing**, turn to 202

You now have some scale considerations. You need to find larger producers, but that's a big hassle.

You take time and resources to expand and strengthen your supply chain, which is great. You identify new producers and co-ops. Then you find new vendors and line up those agreements. You expand your bandwidth of supply.

But you end up spending so much to develop your supply chain that the sales don't support the expense. If you have too much supply and not enough demand, it won't work.

With my honeycomb business, this is by far the largest investment of capital with the longest return on that investment. However, it's entirely necessary to invest in our supply chain to support our purpose. It does pinch our cash flow more than almost any other company I'm aware of. At the beginning, 140 percent of every dollar in sales was going into our supply chain, which does not make for a very sustainable business.

All that said . . .

You have to go back to marketing and sales.

To **invest in marketing**, turn to page 202

Note: If you have been on this page before and are noticing a pattern, turn to page 203 to finish the story.

You Invest in Marketing

You decided to focus on customer relationships, marketing sales, repeat sales, and increasing sales size.

You work smarter and you have more resources at your disposal. You're doing the best you can with what you've got. And unfortunately, what you've got is less than what other people have. And that creates most of the frustration I've personally found: trying to run a company with ideals and values, instead of selling to the biggest buyer. But you manage to find larger buyers, and you want to be able to fulfill bigger orders, but you can't get too far ahead.

For me, marketing is alchemy. It is art. Yes, of course there is science behind it, but it feels like throwing spaghetti on the wall. It took me a year and a half to land on a video ad campaign that actually resonated with the consumer. That is costly but necessary learning.

All that said . . .

To fulfill those orders, you're back to investing in your supply chain.

To **invest in the supply chain**, turn to page 201

Note: If you have been on this page before and are noticing a pattern, turn to page 203 to finish the story.

CONCLUSION

Did you notice the endless loop in this story? That was to demonstrate the reality of what it's like to be a CPG founder at this stage. Your priority is maintaining that delicate balance of supply and demand and of incremental growth.

> *So many founders missed the point. They say, 'I'll save a dollar here and will use it towards marketing,' or 'I will put it all toward product development,' and leave nothing for marketing. This allocation of financial resources versus human time never seems to balance out. It's like the shell game with the shells moving around and you're shifting your dollars.*
>
> **—Matt Matros, founder of Protein Bar, Limitless, and Shopflix Studios**

You do it well and wake up ten years later to find that you are a meaningful entity who has delivered on your promise. It was not easy, and it was not glamorous. It's definitely not glamorous. It's daily, weekly, monthly considerations of compromise and sacrifice.

But you never made a compromise on your product or your vision. Well done!

You pick up a newspaper one day and see your company being described as the top global buyer that has changed the industry and achieved everything you ever could have imagined.

You are a media darling, a household name known for quality ingredients. You have become iconic, and your brand has become synonymous with quality and integrity. And that is everything you've ever set out to be.

In the end, though, it's not about you. It's about the work you do. Your consumers buy your product over and over and over again to support that worthy cause. Your legacy will live on forever, and your company will be a century old, just like you dreamed.

THE
(REAL)
END

EPILOGUE

I hope this book left you with more questions than answers. That you're frustrated and don't know which direction to go. This isn't a "how I did it" tome, as you've realized by now. I'll admit I don't have many of the answers myself most of the time, so I am doing my best with the resources I have to match the aims I have for my own business.

The CPG world might seem straightforward to anyone from the outside—make a product, sell a product. But under that simple exterior lie the endless decisions and mistakes to be made. Decisions of probability are measured against personal desires and a very loud marketplace of "experts" shilling the "best" practices and playbooks to success.

Few founders, if any, nail it on the first go (or second or third, for that matter). Things get ugly. Those who stick to their aims, avoid temptation, and make decisions based on their predetermined desired outcome are the ones who truly win.

Sure, the make-a-product, sell-a-product process can be done efficiently. Once you get those basics handled according to your specific set of circumstances, it's the financial balancing act that becomes the new game. It's all about cash flow to make a product and sell a product. It takes infrastructure and logistics. This isn't tech, so there is a certain amount of scale that has to be achieved within some timeline. I don't know anyone who has infinite time to build their business.

Of course, it's my hope that you voraciously read every single storyline in this book and learned that there tends to be a higher rate of failure when you start slow, such as the farmers' market route. Those who take a cautious, dip-our-toe-in-the-water, see-how-far-we-can-go attitude don't usually last long. While logically easing into things seems to be the right choice, when you don't put the resources behind your company, it's incredibly difficult to achieve scale and profitability while sustaining any momentum.

This is a truth that goes beyond the CPG industry. It applies to industries like apparel, home goods, and beauty items equally. It may be confusing, but if you want your company to be spinning out $1 million a year, it's a long way from the farmers' market table. It will probably cost you $500,000 to $700,000 just to make the product to support that many sales. This doesn't even include other operational costs like staff and marketing!

My purpose for writing this book is to help would-be founders get really clear on their intentions and then put the proper resources behind that intention. That, if anything, is the secret recipe of success. I'm not telling you what your business size or shape or look should be. I'm telling you that once you decide what you want, you need to put the right resources behind that vision to achieve it.

Now that you've finished this book, you know most of the typical areas of failure: pricing, margins that are too low, competitive headwinds, false positives from friends and family, moving too fast, getting too big without underlying financials, not enough funding to support growth, ineffective partners, and the ever-present cash-flow concerns. Step back, calibrate your thinking, and get clear about what you want. Then move accordingly. Don't listen to the noise.

REAL FOUNDERS: STORIES OF SACRIFICE AND SUCCESS

Vanessa Dew, cofounder of Health-Ade

Starting Up

I started a business club with my best friend and her husband because we were interested in business, and it gave us an excuse to have dinner and wine every week. Her husband came home one day distraught because he had been sentenced to baldness by thirty years old. We all decided we should try to cure baldness, so we researched and found out that kombucha has been anecdotally linked to helping with hair loss.

So we started toiling away in our kitchen, brewing and testing cultures as hair masks on his head. Running a clinical trial on hair loss was not one of our core competencies, nor could we fund it, so we said, "Let's just go to a farmers' market, sell kombucha, learn something, maybe recoup some dollars and move on to the next business."

On March 25, 2021, we sold our first bottle of Health-Ade at a farmers' market. We came with sixty bottles that we had made in our kitchen (our biggest run to that point), and we sold out. Because it was not an established category, there was a huge educational element. We knew kombucha existed on the market, but it seemed like nobody else knew. Customers didn't even know how to pronounce it. We had to educate with a message that resonated past the alternative world of granolas and yogis and into the mainstream. Not only did we have to teach people what it was, we wanted them to know we had the best-tasting, highest-quality kombucha available.

We could have continued at farmers' markets and picked up wholesale accounts. We didn't have to push it. But we are all achievers, so we asked, "Is this all our business is going to be?" Our first business plan was that we would hire only two more people in addition to the three of us and then we'd get to $100 million in sales. We were so innocent! Nine years later, we're in all fifty states with over two hundred employees. We've been the fastest-growing brand of kombucha in the category by far.

Sacrifices

Everything seemed hard and everything had a tradeoff. I was single when the business was just getting started, and it was so demanding. Trying to date was very odd. I couldn't devote enough of me to one person because all of me was in the business.

I paid myself last and worst for so long. Sure, you make sacrifices for the greater good of the business, but pay yourself your worth.

Lezlie Karls-Saltarelli, Nick Saltarelli, and Jake Karls, cofounders of Mid-Day Squares

Starting Up

Lezlie: When you found a company, it needs to solve a problem that you have yourself. If it's not designed for you, it won't have the instinctual edge to succeed, in my opinion. I tried designing a clothing line for women with different body types than my own. That didn't work. Customers want to know who the brand comes from and what the brand stands for. That's how you become a strong business. I created Mid-Day Squares for Nick and myself. I knew we needed something else besides candy bars to satisfy that craving for something sweet we always felt halfway through the day. I created something that solved our problem.

One piece of advice I would offer is just do three big things every day. Just take it day by day. In the beginning, we invested very little in the company. We invested only what we needed to get ready to sell the bar.

We took the path of independence and soul. We wanted to build a legacy brand, not just a brand to flip and sell to the highest bidder. When you start, just start. Don't get stuck in your own mind with analysis paralysis. So many people spend too much time thinking about this big plan. You don't even know what is going to happen a week from now, much less six months. Make sure you have a great gross margin or a plan to have one and grow sales. Do this and everything else will work itself out.

Nick: We always say when you find yourself on the side of the majority, stop and reflect. Every time I've tried to make money, I never made money. And every time I didn't try to make money, I made money. Making money shouldn't be the reason you do what you do. We were ridiculed by investors in the beginning because we were showing vulnerability and authenticity, but it got us to our first one thousand true fans and way more now!

Matt Matros, founder of Protein Bar, Limitless, and Shopflix Studios

Starting Up

I always say, "Just do it." Someone has to start somewhere. Might as well be you.

Entrepreneurship's not for everyone. At the end of the day, it takes the first step. That's it. That's the only thing that entrepreneurs do that's different than everybody else. Lots of people have ideas. How many times have you had a friend who's like, "I thought of that three years ago!" Well, the person who did it, did it. They thought of it three years ago too. They just did something about it.

Nothing is ever 100 percent. I hear that so many founders have analysis paralysis. They get crippled at that stage and just give up because they lose hope. They always are trying to talk themselves into things that don't really matter.

Take a long assessment of risk and then decide if you can take it. The likelihood of the worst-case happening in start-ups is pretty high. Everything distills down to two questions: Could I do this despite all of the risk? If it fails, am I OK with it? Every time I start a business I ask myself, "If this fails, am I out on the streets? Will my mom and sister stop loving me? Of course not." Those are my worst-case scenarios.

With that said, founders oftentimes force a solution into a problem. They want to start a business so bad that they just try to solve something that's not really that much of a problem. They don't stop to question if the problem is really that much worse than the existing solution. It has to be a real problem. You can use all the pretty charts and graphs to say this, but consumers have to actually buy.

Limitless was a failure to begin with. I started Limitless as a coffee company, but it wasn't until I did the water with caffeine that it became a success. Many entrepreneurs oftentimes are so stubborn and rigid that they don't want to come off that initial insight, sometimes to their detriment. Since I was going broke and I needed to survive, I needed to do something, so that's when I shifted my product.

Sacrifices

Today I think a lot of founders don't recognize some of the things they're going to have to give up, at least temporarily. I started when I was twenty-nine and I sacrificed many things. I was single without kids so most notably I sacrificed friendships that weren't really friendships. The type of friends that just text you on a Saturday and say, "Hey, let's go to the beach."

I told them, "I'm doing QuickBooks, bro."

They couldn't understand why I wouldn't go.

The second is mental health. That can be a big sacrifice. The axiom is "heavy is the head that wears the crown." It's true—there is a lot of pressure and anxiety that comes with making decisions.

The third is self. It's been said that in our lives we have five forces: self, family, friends, career, and sleep. The rub is that we only have time to do three of them well. You can do all of them, but you can't do them all really well all the time.

As an entrepreneur, typically business is the number one, so then that leaves you two other buckets to fill and it's up to you to choose. In my instance, recently I've sacrificed self and friendships. What that means is exercise, the mental health stuff, other hobbies or interests. I'm kind of an economics nerd, so I do like Harvard Kennedy School Executive Education, but other than that I don't really have too many other hobbies or interests. My friendships have had to fall a little bit by the wayside as I have chosen to prioritize only those friends closest to me.

I have a wife and a newborn, so that's the next bucket I choose to fill, with sleep being the third bucket—and even that is only a modest prioritization. I think about that a lot. My wife makes fun of me because she thinks my "five bucket" rule is just my way of copping out when I try to tell her I'm doing all of it. I'm just not doing all of it well. I sit on the stationary bike, sure, but I'm watching CNBC, so I'm not really having a good workout. It's just not one of my top three buckets right now.

Chris Hunter, founder of Four Loko and Koia

Sacrifices

When I was in my twenties, it was easier to sacrifice things than it is now. I was free to do what I wanted without a boss. All my friends had corporate jobs. But that meant they also had good incomes, great networks, happy hours, and Christmas parties. There's a trade-off. Entrepreneurship can get lonely, especially in the early days. I had no people to hang with at work. You are different than the people who decide to get into the corporate world.

When you're an entrepreneur, trajectory comes with tension. The game doesn't stop. You worry you can't cover payroll this month. You can't take a check yourself sometimes. I would go without before I would let my team do that. There is a toll on your mental health and physical health from the stress.

In the beginning, my stress was expressed in toxic, nonproductive ways. I have learned to do better things now like yoga, meditation, and exercise. Self-care comes with experience.

I recommend getting a community around you, including mentors and peers. Don't live in your own mess and think you're alone.

Cassandra Curtis, cofounder of Once Upon a Farm

Starting Up

I started making fresh baby food in my kitchen in 2013, and I remember that first $3,000 that I put into it. My husband was not very happy. Of course, now he's great with it, but that was the biggest barrier up to that point. I put that $3,000 towards the initial packaging production. At that time, I did everything else for pretty much nothing. It was the bare minimum to make it work and get a product out there.

Sacrifices

For me, sacrifices came in terms of people outside of the business. I was not really there "socially" for the first two years. I just didn't have a lot of time to invest in my friendships. My family too. My family and my husband have been very supportive, especially in those early stages, but I was so busy. And myself. I would have loved to do more exercise and take the time to prepare my food really well and sit down and eat, but it was not like that in the beginning.

There are sacrifices to being fully committed, but if you're not fully committed, investors will very likely see that.

If I were to do it again, I would definitely slow down in general on key decisions, whether that is product launches, bringing on new vendors, hires, giving up certain amounts of equity, etc. However, for Once Upon a Farm, speed to market was a key to our success to being pioneers in the category, so I don't regret the speed we went at it.

Christopher Hesse, founder of Vukoo Nutrition

Starting Up

Just take it one day at a time, little by little. It's easy to criticize something already created. But how hard is it to create something that's never been done? For my business I leveraged everything. I was not wealthy, but I had amazing credit when I started.

My motivating factor is that I want to be able to tell my daughter I didn't give up on Vukoo, even when it was too hard. I can't afford to get fatigued. I use mind tricks sometimes to trick myself psychologically. It's OK to go crazy a little bit and talk to yourself and tell yourself, "You got this." Dream and listen to your music. Do anything you need to do to get motivated and get creative.

REAL FOUNDERS: PARTNERSHIPS

Nine times out of ten, when you bring a partner on, you simply divide and conquer. You take turns wearing every hat. Typically, it's all hands on deck to do what needs to get done, and you scrape by using your ingenuity. You take on some tasks. Your partner takes on other tasks.

This practice will get things to a certain point. But somewhere along the line, there will always be a case where somebody has to put some money in, and it's usually not right down the middle. There will always be a time when somebody is working more than the other. That's life.

Typically, one of two things can go wrong when this happens: either you didn't document things properly, or you never really set clear roles and responsibilities in the first place. In the beginning, this is fine. Things just get done. But this will come back to haunt you when the company starts to take off or when it starts to hemorrhage money.

With hardship or success, things come into question. If it's huge success, someone's going to feel like they've done more work than the other to contribute to that success, and they are probably going to want to be paid more or have a greater ownership.

And if it's hardship, someone will point the finger as to whose fault it was and who is going to fix it. Conversations that should happen on day one now have to happen when there's real money on the table, and that can get ugly. It certainly doesn't make for the best negotiation position. Often people fall into stalemate because they are feeling slighted or undervalued. And chances are, you're both feeling the same way.

Here's something you can count on at this point: every attorney you talk to will say, "You should have done this before you started."

Then the blame game really starts. There is no alignment. One person wants to take over the roles because they can do it better. And tough questions come in, like, "Who puts more money in? Who has more control? If I spend more time, am I going to have more ownership?" Here are some of the founders' experiences.

Cassandra Curtis

I wanted to have a business partner, and I knew that I was looking for someone who could complement my skills. I wanted someone with more of the investment experience and raising capital because I had more of the product development, operations, and marketing experience. I started with a certain business partner and it didn't turn out great. Bringing on a replacement business partner was one of the best decisions I could have made because our skills complemented each other so well. Even bigger than that was the cultural fit of the partnership. I mean you're basically marrying someone. You're working together that closely.

The second partner actually found me. He just reached out to my website probably four times. I had gotten a ton of inquiries at that time because I was doing something really new and innovative. Most of the time I just didn't respond because a lot of times the people reaching out were competitors. But he was very persistent, so I called him back and started what ended up being a series of conversations. There was an immediate connection. We decided to partner without ever even having met in person!

There are always going to be differences of opinion, when one person thinks one thing and the other thinks something else. How do you reconcile that? I'm sure we've all heard the stories where one person says they are all in, but then you know the other person carries 80 percent of the weight. When you have a partner, you need to get clear on those things. Make sure that it feels like a solid fit.

Vanessa Dew

One piece of advice I offer is to be careful who you hire. In the beginning, I hired my best friends and family to help us sell and stock our product. When you're in a working relationship, employer to employee, but also have a personal relationship, it's hard to give objective feedback. Feelings get hurt. I had to let a friend go from that job and we're not friends today. It's sad and unfortunate but that's the trade-off that had to be made.

Nina Jolic

I originally partnered with somebody else a couple of years back. I had the recipes, so we started with the marketing end and registered a business name and domain name. I would do the baking, and she would do the marketing, and we would figure out the rest. She is a professional photographer and she wanted to partner because she loved the cookies and saw a need, as I did, for healthy, gluten-free baked goods. What I really liked was that we were different and we both brought different skill sets into the business.

We went to Douglas and asked for some feedback on getting this business going. He scared the hell out of us! He's like, "Can you spend $750,000 on this? Forget the farmers' markets. Go big or go home."

Douglas was a great advisor because he's been in business for a long time, and while he provided expert knowledge, that wasn't the path we wanted to take. We were determined to go into farmers' markets to ease our way into the business and understand both the rewards and obstacles before making any large investment.

But I had to talk my partner off the ledge. He really shook her confidence. She didn't want to spend that kind of money. So she backed out and I decided to hold off, as I really wanted to have a partner in the business, so nothing happened for a couple of years.

Later, I was at an event and a woman I knew talked about products she wanted to take to farmers' markets and suggested we partner and share the cost. We both had full-time jobs when we started, so this was a side hustle.

When you choose a partner, it has to be somebody who is like-minded and has different strengths. We created a project charter that allowed us to share our objectives so that we were both clear what we were expecting and the areas where we would share responsibility and where we would not. We started doing all the research. We were looking at packaging. We were looking at a commercial kitchen. We were looking at everything. And at the same time, we were thinking about marketing and branding. It was a lot of fun!

My objective was to do this for three to four months just to see if this was a viable business for me. I wanted to be able to afford to send my daughter to college. I wanted to see how long it would take until it could hit a scale that would be a solid income. I'm no longer at the age or stage in life where I want to be living in a basement apartment and riding my bike everywhere. I'm not going to change my lifestyle so drastically to support this business. My partner had different objectives. She wanted to go full force.

I pulled out of the business after a couple of months, but my partner has continued. It was hard and I felt awful that it affected her, but she was understanding, and at the end of the day, it was what I had to do for myself, for my family. I have no regrets.

Chris Hunter

Back when I was twenty-five years old, I had this idea that I was very excited about. I brainstormed it with a couple of my buddies, and they said, "Let's go for it!" So we did. Without ever having a conversation about roles and responsibilities, much less equity splits or other legal rights.

I ended up being fired from my own company because I had no legal rights to go back on. Here was this thing that started out as my baby and it evolved into something so big. They took it and ran.

My advice is when you decide to partner, think through the end from the beginning. Spend time on the legal side of things and have those uncomfortable conversations first. It would have been relatively easy for me in the beginning to figure out the equity split and retain my position as majority owner. But once the company was legally structured and we had some success, I was left staring at a loophole I never knew was there.

I shouldn't have been surprised. An executive coach told us we were a three-headed monster. We were misaligned on so many things. Instead of addressing concerns, we overlooked them and moved on. When you have a new company, the high highs and the low lows will bond or break you. But the middle, steady-state road is when the cracks are exposed.

On the flip side, when I started my second company, I knew the potential legal issues and was aware of how I wanted things structured. This time I went in with an aggressive deal and legal structure from the start, so we could all relax and focus on the company and the work.

Mid-Day Squares Team

Jake said, "We didn't choose to be partners because we're family members. We chose to be partners because we complement each other's skill sets. My expectations weren't very clear when I joined as a third partner. The job description is 'Just be you,' but I didn't know what that meant. I didn't know my identity 100 percent. I thought I had to be some sort of manager, like I was taught in college and business programs. Forcing myself into that role killed me for eight months and the business suffered. Once I dropped that expectation, the magic happened.

"As a partner, you don't need to necessarily love the idea of your business 150 percent right away. Product market fit is OK, but what is really important is that you stay true to yourself and who you are. Humanize your brand, have a soul. A soulless brand can only go so far. Authenticity is the new marketing tool.

"Nick had a past partnership that didn't work out even though the business did. We used what he learned from that. From day one, we decided we would always go to a business therapist to hash out business problems and learn how to communicate. If we hadn't, we would not be in business together. We work hard every week in that safe zone to have those hard conversations we need to have. Our organization as a whole has benefited from working on that. This has been the best investment we ever made to date!"

Nick added, "So many of us are just ready to verbalize, and we get stuck not being able to communicate. Research from Y Combinator has shown that of all the failed businesses in their portfolio, 87 percent had founder conflict as the reason for the failure. Ego and resentment emerge when you avoid hard conversations, so we needed to make sure we were communicating together and with our organization as a whole. This helped us develop a high level of trust so we could work independently for the good of the company without worrying about stepping on each other's toes."

ACKNOWLEDGMENTS

Thanks to everyone at Kevin Anderson and Associates, particularly to Kevin. Thanks for buying more time when I shortchanged the first version of the manuscript and for lining up a publisher to pursue this little weird dream of a pick-your-path book.

Thanks to everyone at BenBella Books. Matt Holt, I'm super stoked you captured the idea of a pick-your-path book and wanted to pursue it with a business mindset. It's good to have a publisher who believes in the concept of the format even before the substance, so thanks for taking a chance on this. Thanks to Jessika Rieck for your stellar graphic design chops and tenacity to get it just right, and to Katie Dickman for the clarity and guidance you provided. Thanks to Scott Calamar for your discerning and refining eye on the copyediting front.

Thanks to Jenn Able for being my right hand and my sounding board throughout this whole Pass the Honey journey. And not to ever forget Brittany Callahan for a proofread that clarified thinking and worked through pathways, and ultimately tightened and improved the entire manuscript. Thank you both.

Thanks to Heidi Scott, the saving grace for this whole thing. There would not be a book without you. I absolutely would have given the advance back had you not been here to assist. I was on that fence, so thank you for stepping in and for being the amazing human you are.

Thanks to every one of the wonderful founders that we interviewed for this book. Thank you for the openness and the candor. Sometimes it's not fun to rehash the lumps that we all earn along the way, but for you all to be self-aware enough to understand them and how they affected you, and then to understand that others can gain from your lessons, has strengthened our collective wisdom. Your contribution makes the book real. Heidi and I could have written narrative all day and every day, but it wouldn't have been real. Your stories are what gave that color to anchor this entire book in some reality.

I owe a debt of gratitude to the tens of thousands of founders who have pitched me for funding and shared their stories of success and failure over the decades. To those whom I either have responded to or haven't. To those I invested in and those that I passed on. To the investors who invested in me and those who passed on me. To the entire ecosystem of fundraising and operations. It's an exhaustive number of people, but it's what has allowed me to learn from all of you to actually run Pass the Honey with some measure of decency.

Finally, thank you to founders like Suzy Batiz at Poo-Pourri, Yvon Chouinard at Patagonia, and Hamdi Ulukaya at Chobani.

These are some of the companies that blazed a trail and went against some pretty considerable headwinds, from naming a company with the word "poo" in it, to really reinvesting in the supply chain and redefining two industries at once, to introducing a foreign category of yogurt to the US consumer while championing social responsibility and positive environmental change. These are some of the folks I really admire. Thank you for setting an example for founders like me.

ABOUT THE AUTHOR

Photo by Anna Clevenger

DOUGLAS RAGGIO managed $100M+ marketing campaigns for Fortune 500 companies including Nike, Motorola, DirecTV, and Discovery Channel. As his first venture into the food and beverage space, he founded the slow-cooked meal company Stews & Such, through which he cultivated a network of manufacturers, vendors, distributors, co-packers, and retailers in and around the packaged food space. This experience exposed a gap in the financing options available to emerging brands.

With a focus on food and beverage, Douglas raised and managed an early-growth venture fund, Gastronome Ventures; advised a dozen buy-side transactions; and consulted on more than three dozen sell-side fundraisers.

He is the founder of Bias & Blind Spots, a holding company utilizing a hybrid of debt and equity to provide long-term capital to earlier-stage companies backed by family offices and private investors.

However, his life's work is Pass the Honey, a single-serve, pre-cut, convenience "snacking honey" company. He says, "I never would have thought that peddling honeycomb would turn into what it is. It captures every bit of myself."

Pass the Honey reinvests a sizable amount of profits back into pollinator research and habitat restoration. It also works with fair-trade standards and practices and is setting quality standards and testing standards in the highly fraudulent category of liquid honey. The goal of Pass the Honey is to change the narrative of honey and educate the consumer with the novelty of the honeycomb. It is setting the tone for the entire industry.

Douglas received a BS in organizational communication from Cal Poly Pomona. He is California born and raised, currently residing in Encinitas, with global citizen ambitions.